Building Flickr
Applications with PHP

Rob Kunkle, Andrew Morton

Apress®

Building Flickr Applications with PHP

Copyright © 2006 by Rob Kunkle, Andrew Morton

ISBN-13: 978-1-59059-612-8

ISBN-13 (electronic): 978-1-4302-0221-9

Printed and bound in the United States of America (POD)

Lead Editor: Matthew Moodie
Technical Reviewer: Christian Weiske
Editorial Board: Steve Anglin, Ewan Buckingham, Gary Cornell, Jason Gilmore, Jonathan Gennick,
    Jonathan Hassell, James Huddleston, Chris Mills, Matthew Moodie, Dominic Shakeshaft, Jim Sumser,
    Keir Thomas, Matt Wade
Project Manager: Kylie Johnston
Copy Edit Manager: Nicole LeClerc
Copy Editor: Hastings Hart
Assistant Production Director: Kari Brooks-Copony
Production Editor: Lori Bring
Compositor: Lynn L'Heureux
Proofreader: Linda Seifert
Indexer: John Collin
Cover Designer: Kurt Krames
Manufacturing Director: Tom Debolski

Distributed to the book trade worldwide by Springer-Verlag New York, Inc., 233 Spring Street, 6th Floor, New York, NY 10013. Phone 1-800-SPRINGER, fax 201-348-4505, e-mail orders-ny@springer-sbm.com, or visit http://www.springeronline.com.

For information on translations, please contact Apress directly at 2855 Telegraph Avenue, Suite 600, Berkeley, CA 94705. Phone 510-549-5930, fax 510-549-5939, e-mail info@apress.com, or visit http://www.apress.com.

The source code for this book is available to readers at http://www.apress.com in the Source Code section.

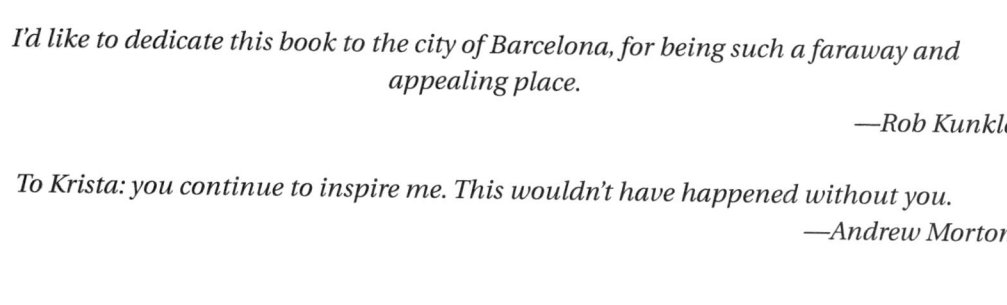

I'd like to dedicate this book to the city of Barcelona, for being such a faraway and appealing place.

—Rob Kunkle

To Krista: you continue to inspire me. This wouldn't have happened without you.

—Andrew Morton

Contents at a Glance

Contents

About the Authors

ROB KUNKLE has been a programmer and general computer enthusiast since he first got his index fingers on a Commodore 64. More recently, he makes a living as a consultant, both putting together applications and taking them apart. He loves a good airy discussion about semantics, causality, artificial intelligence, or just general wild speculation about the future.

He has a passion for photography; he enjoys trying to highlight the unspoken truths and covert beauty found in everyday events and overlooked things. If you ever happen to find yourself sitting in a café in the Inner Sunset district of San Francisco, be sure to sit by the window and daydream; he might just stroll by with his dog and snap your photo. You can see some of his images on Flickr under the screen name *goodlux*.

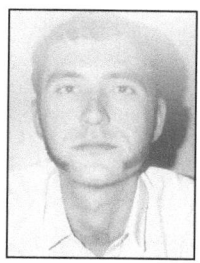

ANDREW MORTON is a longtime student in Portland, Oregon. He enjoys programming, riding bikes, and taking photos in equal measures. Andrew also likes being mistaken for the famous Linux developer and Princess Di's biographer. Andrew is the author of the Phlickr library to access Flickr's API from PHP. You can find his photos on Flickr under the username *drewish*.

About the Technical Reviewer

CHRISTIAN WEISKE is a student of Information Technologies in Leipzig, Germany. He has been a member of the PHP-GTK documentation team for several years, and is a regular contributor to the PEAR project. In his spare time, he works on various PHP-GTK2 tools, translates programs into his native German language, and writes articles for PHP magazines. He also works as a freelancer, creating PHP-GTK applications for those who need some.

You can reach him by email at cweiske@cweiske.de or at his website at www.cweiske.de.

Acknowledgments

We'd like to thank everyone at Apress for their patience and support while working on this book. This book absolutely could not have been written if it weren't for the consistent, considerate, and thorough prompting from Kylie Johnston. Nor would it have been possible without the level-headed and accurate editorial support from Matt Moodie. We'd also like to thank Dan Dofter for his frequent reminders of the wild lifestyle of established tech book authors. Finally, special thanks to Beth Christmas for pushing the ship from the shore by providing the spark of possibility that made this book a reality. We hope to see her novel on shelves someday soon.

Introduction

This book explores some of the interesting things you can do with Flickr by using the PHP programming language. We hope this book makes the Flickr API more accessible to a wider range of users.

Who This Book Is For

This book is intended for photographers, bloggers, and web designers who would like to make greater use of the photos that they have stored on Flickr. We'll introduce you to Flickr, the premier web photo-sharing service, and show you how to use PHP to write scripts to manage and to access your photos, and to make them visible on your personal website.

How This Book Is Structured

This book provides you with everything you need to use PHP to connect to Flickr and make use of its photos.

We begin the book with some quick background on PHP and Flickr in Chapter 1. We take you on an overview of the Flickr website in Chapter 2 and look at some of the things you can do with Flickr out of the box. In Chapter 3 we show you how to set up a development environment so you can start programming with PHP and use all the examples in the book. In Chapter 4, we go over the basics of the PHP language that you will need to be able to work with Flickr. Once you are familiar with the basics, we guide you through how to use Flickr photos (Chapter 5), photosets (Chapter 6), tags (Chapter 7), RSS feeds (Chapter 8), and groups (Chapter 9).

Prerequisites

To get the most out of this book, you'll need to have a PC or Mac that you can set up as a local web server and that can run PHP. You also need to set up a free Flickr account and have some photos to upload.

In the setup chapter we'll walk through installing the Apache 2 web server, the PHP 5 programming language, and the Phlickr package. The book assumes that you'll be running a modern version of either Windows or Linux, but because all the referenced software is relatively platform independent, it should be usable on most other operating systems.

Downloading the Code

To download the sample code, visit the book's home page on the Apress website
(http://www.apress.com) and select Source Code.

Contacting the Authors

Rob Kunkle: rob@goodlux.org, http://www.goodlux.org
Andrew Morton: drewish@katherinehouse.com, http://www.drewish.com

CHAPTER 1

Some Background Notes on Flickr, PHP, and Phlickr

PHP is by far the most popular web scripting language. It's simple to learn, versatile, well documented, and readily available. Flickr is the world's most innovative photo-sharing site. This book is about combining the two to help you build more interesting websites, and to manage and to present your photos.

In the chapters that follow, you'll learn the basics of PHP, how to set up a web development environment, and how to use PHP to access and to present the photos you have stored on the Flickr site.

If you've never used PHP before, or if you still don't have a Flickr account, you won't be left in the dust. The first few chapters give you all the information you need to feel comfortable using Flickr, reading PHP code, and setting up a website on your home computer.

If you're already familiar with PHP, this book will serve as a good quick-start guide to using the PHP Phlickr library, which allows you to communicate with Flickr. This book will also have you working with the Flickr application program interface (API) in no time. You might want to jump ahead to Chapter 5 and have a look at some of the examples.

What Is So Special About Flickr?

There are a lot of photo-sharing sites out on the web. If you've never used Flickr (http://www.flickr.com) or visited the site only once or twice, you might not see any great differences other than a slightly more confusing interface. Yet Flickr is often touted as a poster child of Web 2.0 technologies.

Note *Web 2.0* is a very loosely defined term that is sometimes used to describe websites that employ the latest, novel techniques and practices. These sites generally emphasize collaboration, social networks, open programming interfaces, and machine-readable interfaces. But on a deeper level, Web 2.0 is meant to embody the zeitgeist of the Internet, as it were: the websites, people, and ideas that are most representative of what the web is about today. In much the same way that the world of the '80s was very different from that of the '60s, and Generation Xers are different from the Baby Boomers, the virtual world of today has a very different look, feel, and personality from the virtual world of the '90s. The concept of Web 2.0 expresses this sea change nicely.

What makes Flickr different than other image-storage sites is the emphasis on openness, collaboration, social networking, and innovation. Features such as the open API; collaborative tagging; and cool, flashy interfaces set Flickr apart from the pack. These features also make Flickr much more useful from the standpoint of a programmer or blogger.

We'll take a detailed look at Flickr's features in the next chapter, but for now, let's look at some background on Flickr and PHP.

The Game That Never Ends: A Short History of Flickr

One of the major appeals of the Flickr website is its playfulness. Perhaps this is because at heart, Flickr is a game.

Flickr has its roots in the massive, multiplayer, online game called Game Neverending, or GNE for short. GNE was a completely web-based game from Ludicorp (http://www. ludicorp.com) in which you could share game objects and interact with other users through an instant-messaging interface. So you could, for instance, swap a massage ticket or a glass of limeade with another player, or take some virtual slack. It wasn't a far stretch for the developers to realize that in addition to game objects, it would also be fun to share other digital objects, such as a PDF file, a Word document, or . . . a photo (Figure 1-1).

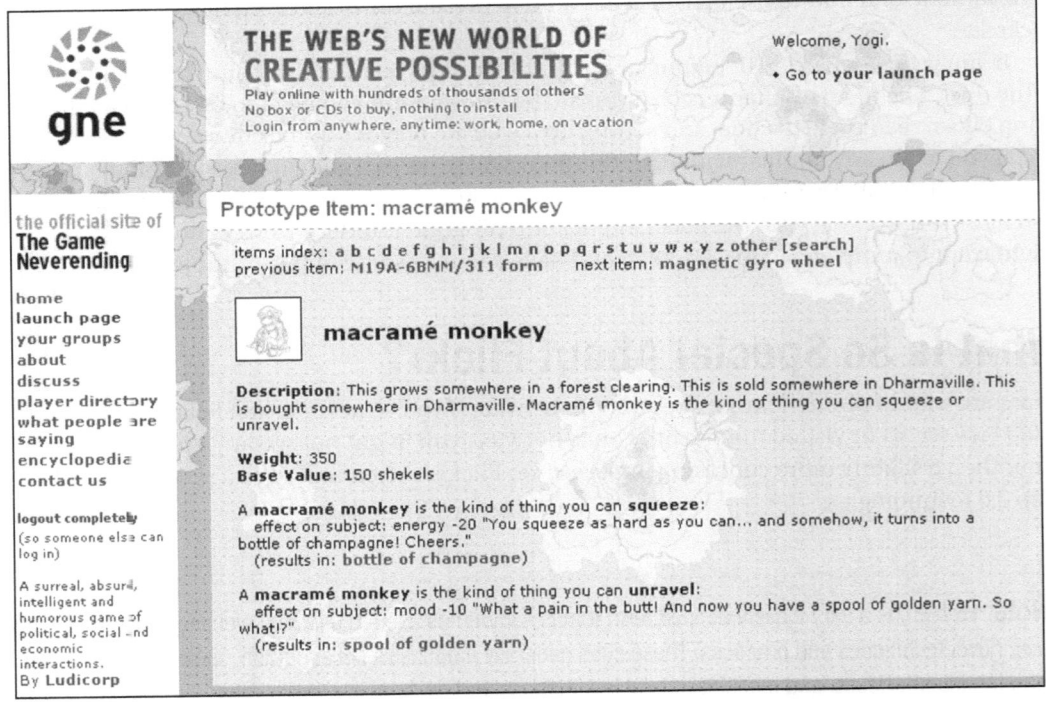

Figure 1-1. *The macramé monkey was an object that could be shared in GNE.*

The official Flickr site went live in February of 2004. In its earliest incarnation, Flickr was really just a stripped-down version of the GNE interface. You could upload photos and store them in your personal "shoebox," then drag the photos into a chat window to discuss them with others.

As the Flickr site grew, development turned towards a more asynchronous model, where comments would live on the site as HTML pages, rather than just fleeting conversation in a chat room. So a photo could build up a comment history over time. This worked well for bloggers, who needed a place where they could store their bulky 8-megapixel photos. The original chat functionality eventually became just one feature of the site, called Flickr Live, then was phased out.

Another feature that was added in after the initial launch was tagging (Figure 1-2). This extremely popular feature allows you to categorize photos with any words you choose. Taken on its own, this may not seem like a terribly interesting feature, but when you mix in the tags of thousands of other users in an open system like Flickr, a novel phenomenon emerges. Out of the combined chaos of individuals tagging photos with whatever words they please comes a sort of cultural classification system, sometimes called a *folksonomy*, where you can actually see what a word means to everyone using the system. This is great for exploring what a word or group of words means to our whole culture. It's especially telling to look up words with more nebulous meanings, such as *love*, *fear*, or *whoops*.

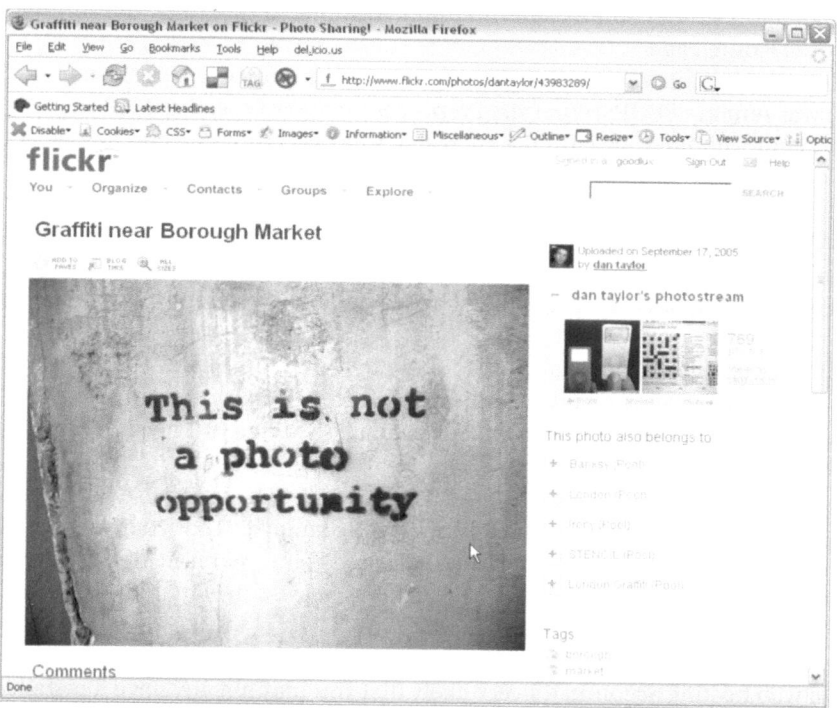

Figure 1-2. *Photo tagged with irony. Creative Commons Licensed Photo by Dan Taylor. Graffiti by Unknown.*

A year after Flickr's initial launch, rumors started circulating that Yahoo! was interested in acquiring Ludicorp. Sure enough, in March of 2005, Yahoo! bought Ludicorp. While initially this met with some resistance from the user base, Flickr had grown to the point where it was frequently "having a massage" (down for servicing), and it's now generally accepted that the union with Yahoo! added to the overall stability of the site.

Game Neverending was eventually put aside as the popularity of the photo-sharing component of the game grew. While GNE now appears to be permanently on the shelf, if you look closely at the address bar while moving through the Flickr site, you might catch a glimpse of the spirit of the game still alive and well, encoded in the URLs: `http://flickr.com/groups_admin.gne?id=14157979@N00`.

The name Flickr also has a colorful history. According to Flickr developer Eric Costello, the name Flicker was first thought up in the back of an '86 Ford Econoline van by co-developer and philosopher Ben Cerveny on a trip to the airport. The innovative *sans e*–style name was thought up by Caterina Fake when they found that Flicker.com was already taken. Conveniently, this opened up a whole world of names for third-party Flickr applications, such as Mappr, Uploadr, and Organizr.

PHP Background

PHP (`http://www.php.net`) has its humble beginning as a set of scripts created by Rasmus Lerdorf in 1995 to manage a simple home page and online résumé. At that time, the acronym PHP stood for Personal Home Page.

By 1997, the code was completely rewritten by Andi Gutmans and Zeev Suraski, and the first official version was renamed PHP: Hypertext Preprocessor and released as PHP 3.

Further releases came in mid-1999 with PHP 4, which was based on the Zend engine, and more recently PHP 5 in 2004.

While the language has come a long way since the initial scripts created 11 years ago, in one sense it remains true to its roots: PHP is still a great language for putting together a simple website. You can easily write a bit of PHP code inside of HTML tags and have a page that changes every time you view it, or connect to a database to pull out stored information to display to users.

In the following chapters, we'll show you how to pull random photos from Flickr, batch-edit tags and titles, display your photo sets on your own website, display information culled from Flickr groups, and much more. This book will give you all the tools you need to make use of the full Flickr API.

If you are considering whether or not to take the time to learn PHP, as opposed to another language, we highly recommend it. It's an extremely accessible language that you can pick up quickly, yet it is full featured and scales well to handle extremely large, complicated tasks. How large? How complicated? To give you and idea of what is possible, you need to look no further than the Flickr site itself, which is written mainly in PHP.

As added pluses, PHP is well documented, has a massive user base, and is very accessible. If you already have a web hosting account, it's very likely that you may already have it installed.

We will cover the basics of PHP so that you can interact with Flickr, but for a more comprehensive tutorial, we suggest you read *Beginning PHP and MySQL 5: From Novice to Professional* by W. Jason Gilmore (ISBN 1-59059-552-1; Apress, 2006). If you haven't already, we also highly recommend that you take a look at the official PHP website at `http://www.php.net`. As mentioned before, the language is extremely well documented on the site, and the documentation is constantly updated.

About Phlickr

Throughout this book we will be using the Phlickr PHP 5 libraries developed by co-author Andrew Morton. The Phlickr libraries act as a bridge between PHP and the Flickr API. Phlickr does the hard work of sending requests to the Flickr web server and making Flickr's responses available to PHP, and it generally makes the programming more fun. Instead of spending time writing your own PHP code to talk to the Flickr server directly, you can make use of well-designed and well-thought-out Phlickr objects to get right to your photos, sets, and groups.

Like PHP, the Phlickr libraries are also well documented. You can find the latest detailed information about all of the Phlickr objects at the Phlickr API reference: `http://www.drewish.com/projects/phlickr/docs/`.

Summary

We've had a quick look through the history of Flickr and PHP in this chapter, in anticipation of the rest of the book. Now that you know a little bit about Flickr and PHP, we should get started. In the next chapter we'll take an in-depth look at Flickr's features. Then we'll cover the installation of PHP in Chapter 3 and the basics in Chapter 4.

CHAPTER 2

∎∎∎

Flickr Features

Flickr is truly the Swiss Army Knife of photo-sharing sites. You can use it in so many ways that all of the features might seem overwhelming to a first-time user. In this chapter we will walk through the basics of using Flickr and focus on the core functionality. Our goal is to take a wide view of all the ways that you might want to use Flickr for your own photos and to survey the possibilities.

Hello, Aloha, G'day, Namaste, Hoi, Hala, Hola

Before you can use Flickr, you will first need to create an account with Yahoo!, Flickr's parent company. To do this, simply point your browser to `http://www.flickr.com` and click the red "Sign up!" button on the right-hand side of the screen. You will be asked to fill out a few basic pieces of information and to agree to the terms of service.

Once you've created your account and you first log on to Flickr, you will be greeted by a headline that says "hi" in one of many languages, reflecting the global nature of the Flickr site and its users (Figure 2-1).

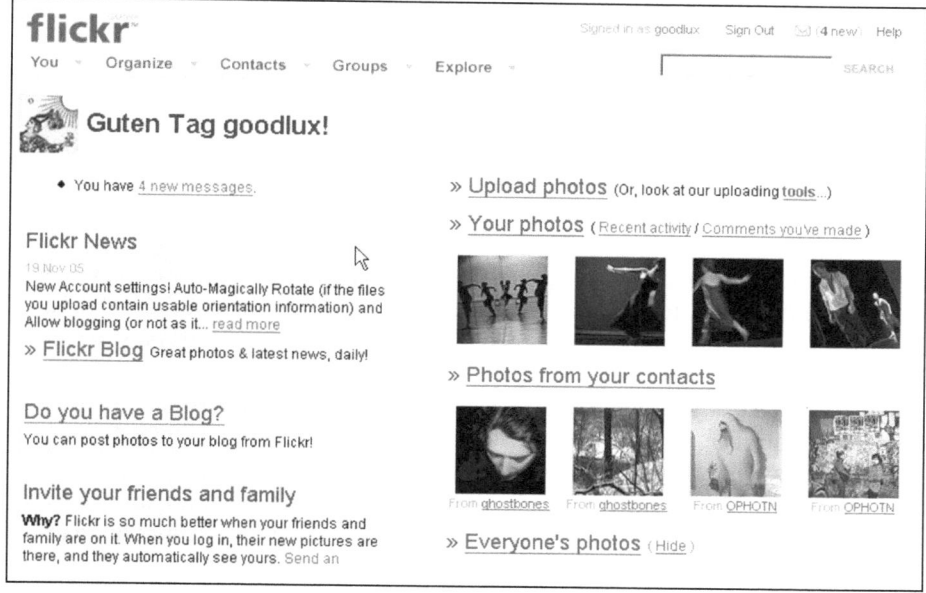

Figure 2-1. *Flickr home page*

Next to the greeting you see your own icon, which by default is a stodgy, humdrum, blocky face (Figure 2-2).

Figure 2-2. *Stodgy icon*

You'll probably want to change that to something more representative right away. Perhaps a photo of yourself or an image of something you hold close to your heart. Doing this is simple. Hover your cursor over your buddy icon, open the context menu using the arrow that appears, and click the Your Buddy Icon link. You will be taken to the screen shown in Figure 2-3.

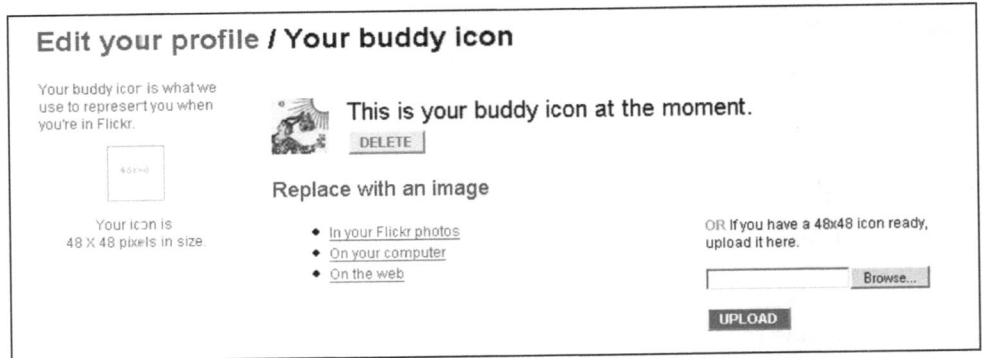

Figure 2-3. *Editing your buddy icon*

Next you'll need an image to use. Flickr will resize any image you give it to 48×48 pixels, so you don't have to fret if your image isn't cropped to the right size, but you'll want to pick an image that is pretty much square in shape. You have four options as far as where the actual image comes from. If you've already uploaded some photos, you can pick an image from your photostream (more on photostreams in the Photostreams and Syndication Feeds section). Otherwise, you can provide Flickr with a URL of an image that is out on the web somewhere, you can choose an image on your computer, or you can just click Browse and select a ready-made 48×48 image on your computer. Once you've done this, you will notice that the gray blockhead is gone and has been replaced with your new image.

Now that your account has a little more personality, you might want to go and have a look at some of your account options. To do so, click on You ➤ Your Account link at the top of the page. The "Your account" page is the central control panel for all of the settings on your account (Figure 2-4).

From here you can make adjustments to the way your photos are displayed, who's allowed to see them, and how they are licensed. You can also set up a blog or blogs that you will be sending photos to and get an email address to use for photo uploads. You can use the privacy settings to control how your personal information is displayed and add more information about yourself to your profile. We'll explore these options in greater detail, but for the moment, let's flip back to your home page by clicking the You link in the upper-left corner of the page.

Your account
You have a Flickr Pro Account. It expires on 2nd February, 2009.
You can extend your Pro Account here, or view your order history.
Photo Settings
Uploading Tools
We have a number of uploading tools that you can install on your computer to do batch photo uploads.
Uploading by email
Did you know you can email your pictures directly into your photostream in Flickr? Or post directly to your moblog by email?
Default Photo Privacy
Specify who can see your photos at a default level. This will apply to all the photos you upload to Flickr.
Allowing Downloads
Configure who can see the option to download larger versions of your photos.
Privacy Settings
Notifications from Flickr
You can control how and when you receive email notifications from Flickr.
Your privacy
You can control how much of your profile information shows to people who use Flickr.
Personal Information
Your profile
Tell people a little (or a lot) about yourself.
(Or, view your profile page as it looks to everyone else.)
Your Yahoo! preferences
This is just a handy link for Yahoo! peeps to get to your Y! preferences

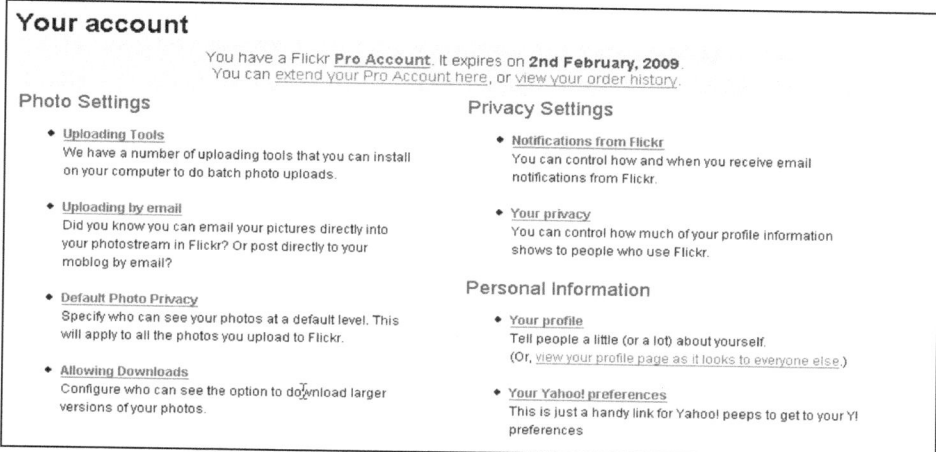

Figure 2-4. *Your account settings*

Adding Photos

Now that you've customized your account, you will want to upload some photos. The most straightforward way to do this is by clicking You ➤ Upload Photos. This will take you to the "Upload photos to Flickr" page (Figure 2-5).

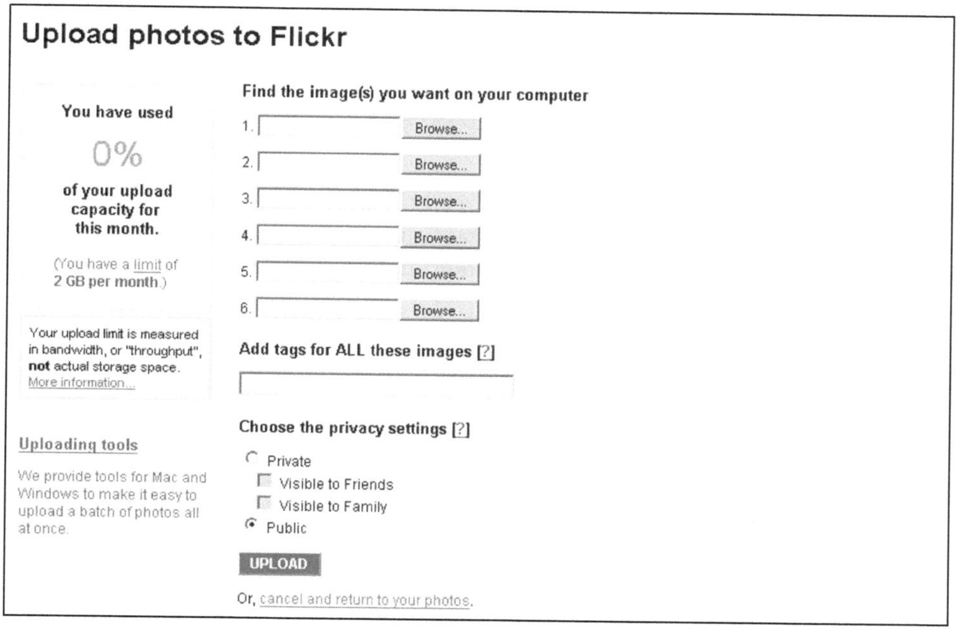

Upload photos to Flickr
You have used
0%
of your upload capacity for this month.
(You have a limit of 2 GB per month.)
Your upload limit is measured in bandwidth, or "throughput", not actual storage space.
More information...
Uploading tools
We provide tools for Mac and Windows to make it easy to upload a batch of photos all at once.
Find the image(s) you want on your computer
1. Browse...
2. Browse...
3. Browse...
4. Browse...
5. Browse...
6. Browse...
Add tags for ALL these images [?]
Choose the privacy settings [?]
Private
Visible to Friends
Visible to Family
Public
UPLOAD
Or, cancel and return to your photos.

Figure 2-5. *Individual upload screen*

Click the Browse button and select an image file from your computer to upload. You can repeat this several times if you have a few files that you want to upload. You can also tag these photos by writing in a few descriptive words to categorize the photos. (We'll look at tagging in greater detail in the "Tagging Photos" section later in this chapter.) Once you've located your photos, click UPLOAD to begin sending your photos to Flickr.

You are probably going to want to upload more that just a few photos at a time. Fortunately, Flickr offers an array of third-party tools for managing your uploads from different platforms. If you are using a Mac or Windows, you can use Uploadr (Figure 2-6).

Figure 2-6. *Uploading with Uploadr*

Uploadr allows you to drag and drop photos directly from your file system or iPhoto to a window for uploading. You also have the option of tagging the photos that you are uploading, setting permissions (more on that in the "Sharing Your Photos" section), and resizing the photos on the fly.

Also available for the Windows XP platform is a shell extension that allows you to simply right-click the photo in the Windows Explorer to upload it. You can download this extension and Uploadr from the download tools page at http://www.flickr.com/tools/.

If you are using a Mac, in addition to Uploadr, you can use an application called "1001" or a plug-in for iPhoto to manage your uploads. If you are using a recent Nokia camera phone, you can post to Flickr via Lifeblog. You simply enter a few details into your phone and you are ready to go.

A final cross-platform option for uploading is to upload by email. Flickr gives each person a customized email address that they can send photos to. This means any operating system or camera phone that supports emails can also be used to send photos to Flickr. You can get an upload email address at http://www.flickr.com/account/uploadbyemail/. Again, more information on all of these upload options can be found on the Flickr website at http://www.flickr.com/tools/.

Photostreams and Syndication Feeds

If you are on the home page, and you click your browser's Reload button, you will notice that the photos displayed under Everyone's Photos change with each reload. At first glance this might appear to be a random sampling of some of the photos stored in the Flickr site. What you are actually seeing, though, is a window into the photos that were currently being uploaded to Flickr at the very moment you clicked Reload. In other words, you are looking at the latest photos in the Flickr photostream.

Flickr revolves around the concept of the photostream. Each time you upload an image it is added to your own personal photostream in the order it is uploaded. Additionally, your image will appear in the global photostream, instantly visible to users all over the world. See for yourself—upload a photo, then click on the Everyone's Photos link from the home page. If you look through the images, you will see the image you just uploaded, along with photos from everyone else, in the order they were added to the site.

In addition to the pages you see in your browser on the Flickr site, photostreams are also published to the web using standardized syndication formats. Really Simple Syndication (RSS) is probably the most well known of these syndication formats. RSS is a machine-readable XML format that can be used to publish all kinds of information to the web, such as weblogs, news sites, and even podcasts. When information is published using a syndication standard, such as RSS, it is called a feed. So a photostream is also a feed.

If you want an idea of what a feed actually looks like, click the You link. If you scroll all the way to the bottom of the page, you will see a link that reads "Feed." If you click this, you will see the XML file that makes up an RSS feed (Figure 2-7).

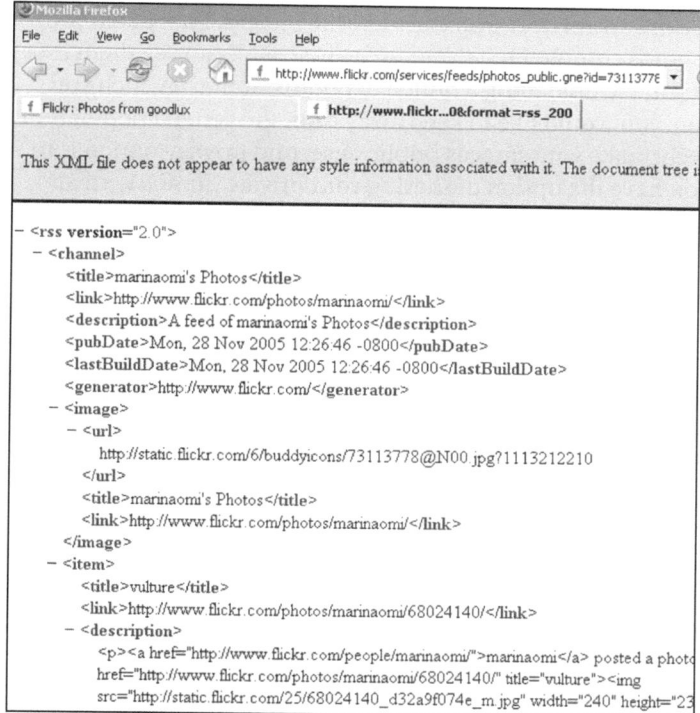

Figure 2-7. *An RSS feed viewed in the browser*

To make use of feeds you use an application called an aggregator. Aggregators allow you to select different feeds from the web and have them all available in one place. You can subscribe to your favorite newspapers, blogs, and photostreams; easily browse through them; and be notified the minute something new is posted. This is a great way to view the latest photos from your Flickr friends and contacts, and to see them the minute they are posted. If you are using Windows, RSS Bandit (http://www.rssbandit.org) or SharpReader (http://www.sharpreader.net) are good choices for free aggregators. Try them out.

Note We'll see more on feeds in Chapters 8 and 9.

Sharing Your Photos

Flickr is all about sharing photos. If you want to make your photos accessible to anyone and everyone in the world, it's very easy. You can do this while you are uploading photos: simply select Public from the privacy options, and your photos will be available to others all over the world the moment they upload. If your photo is particularly fetching, it's not uncommon for people to leave their comments about the photo seconds after you have uploaded it. Flickr is definitely the way to go if you want a massive audience for your photos.

Perhaps you aren't that much of an exhibitionist and you want to fine-tune your exposure a bit. Flickr gives you another choice: making your photos private. When you make your photos private, you get a finer degree of control over who can view the images. First of all, you have the option of making the photos completely private, so no one at all can see them except yourself. This is a good choice if you are uploading a bunch of photos, some of which you would like to be public and others you would like to keep away from the general population. After uploading you can selectively make your images public. A second privacy option is to make the photos semiprivate. You have the option of sharing your private photos with an inner circle of friends, your family, or both.

In order to take advantage of the friends and family options, you will need to invite them to check out your photostream, and they will need to join Flickr. To do this, you can click the Contacts ➤ Invite your Friends link. Enter the names and email addresses of the people you'd like to invite, and check off whether they are friends or family (or just a contact).

When they receive your email and check out your photos, they will automatically be listed on your contacts page. You can get to this page by clicking the Contacts link.

Annotating Photos

Whoever said a picture is worth a thousand words surely never had to find one particular image in a database of millions. Sometimes a single word connected to a photo can be much more valuable than all the photos in a shoebox.

Flickr gives you lots of ways that you can add text to your photos to describe them and make them searchable. Let's look at these options now.

Titles and Descriptions

When you upload a photo, its default title is the original file name of the image. You probably want to come up with a more flavorful title than something like DCIM_0921. Changing the title is very straightforward. Click on the thumbnail of the photos you want to edit to go to the individual photo page. Click on the title, type in your new title, and click the SAVE button. Adding a description is equally easy. Just click on the area under the photo, write a little more about your photo, and click SAVE. You can also add a comment here.

You'll notice that there is an area on the page to enter tags. We will look at tags in more detail a little further on in this chapter, but for now, feel free to enter a few words to describe or categorize the photo: perhaps a friend's name, an event, or the camera you used to take the picture.

If you have a lot of photos that you want to title and describe but you don't feel like clicking through each photo individually, you can edit the photos as a batch. Click the You link near the top of the page. This will bring you to the "Your photos" page, where you can see the latest view of your photostream. Here you can click on and edit the titles and descriptions as you could in an individual photo's page. You can't, however, add comments. Make the changes you want, and don't forget to click SAVE for each photo you edit.

Notes

Now that you've given titles and descriptions to some photos, let's take a look at another way you can add information to your photos: using notes. Arguably one of the coolest interface features of Flickr is the ability to select a portion of the photo and attach a note to it. Click on any photo thumbnail to go to the individual photo page. Along the top of the photo, just under the title, you will see a selection of icons. Click the ADD NOTE icon (Figure 2-8).

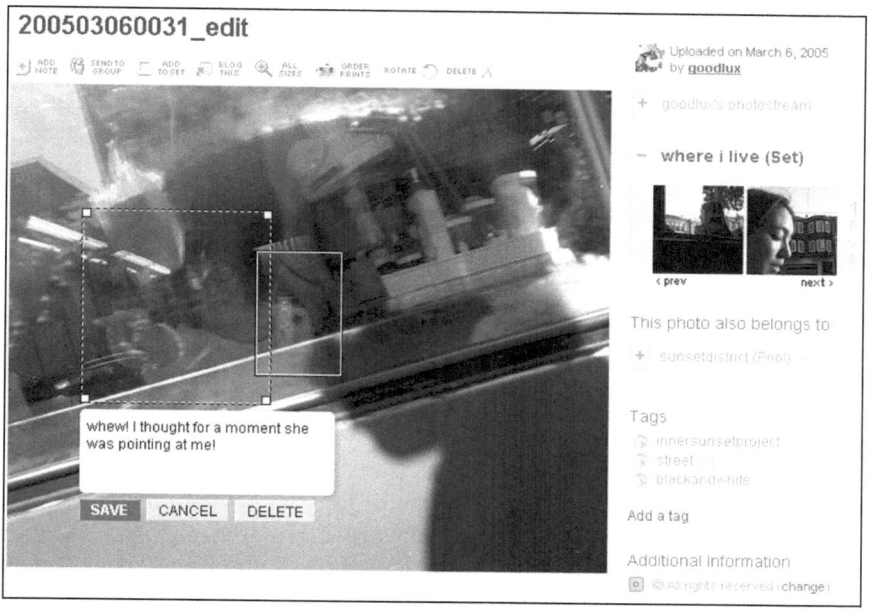

Figure 2-8. *Adding a note to an image*

A small box and area to write a note appears. Use the corners of the box to select a portion of your photo, then type your note into the text area. When you've finished, click SAVE, and there you have it, your new note. Now when someone else looks at your photo, they will be able to see the note and the area of the photo that you've drawn their attention to.

Unlike titles and descriptions, which only you can edit, photos are a collaborative feature, so others can leave notes on your images if you allow it. By default, your contacts, friends, and family are allowed to leave notes. If you want to change this setting, you can do so from the You ➤ Your Account ➤ Default Photo Privacy page.

Comments

Another collaborative feature for annotating photos is the comments feature. Using comments, you can keep a running commentary on your photos, and let others in on what you think of their work. If you scroll down to the bottom of any individual photo page, you will see an area to add comments. Most people love to get response from the work they've posted, so don't be timid; if you see something you like, be sure to take a moment to let the photographer know you like their work.

Favorites

In addition to writing a glowing review of a photo in the comments, another way you can let someone know that you love their work is by making it a favorite. To do this, you click the ADD TO FAVES star icon above that perfect photo.

When clicked, the star changes from clear to pink (Figure 2-9) and is now one of your favorites. To see all of your favorites grouped together, click the You ➤ Your Favorites link. After you've been out picking your favorite images for a while, you might be surprised at what a stunning collection you've put together. It's a very good way to learn something about yourself.

Figure 2-9. *The favorites icon*

You can also view other people's favorite photos. This is great way to get to know the tastes of other users, as well as to locate some of the best images that Flickr has to offer. To get to another user's favorites, click on the hyperlink of the user's name. This will take you to a page that is almost exactly the same as the "Your photos" page except that it is the other user's photos. At the top, you will see the Favorites link. Click that to see all of the other person's favorite photos.

Recent Activity

If you want to see the comments, notes, and tags that people have left on your own photos, as well as your images that have been added to someone's favorites, click the Activity ➤ On Your Photos link at the bottom of the page. From the "Recent activity on your photos" page you can select a time frame and see all of the latest activity on your work (Figure 2-10).

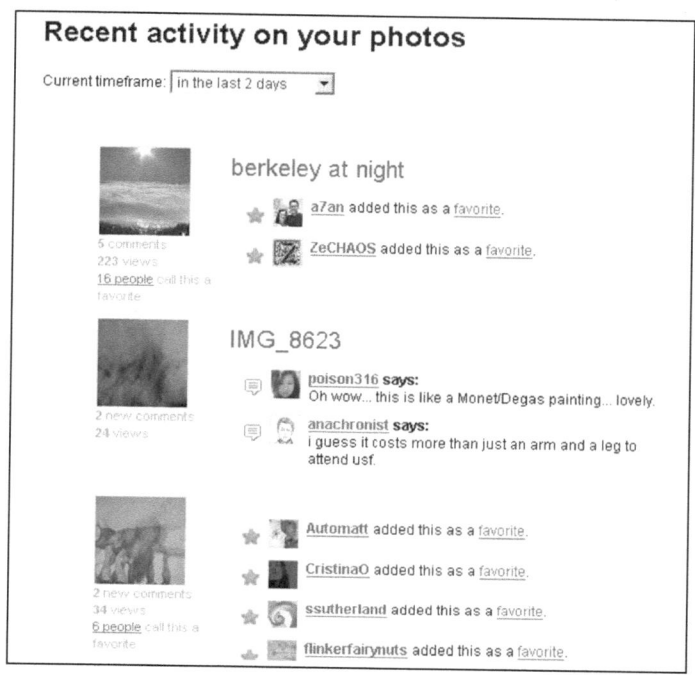

Figure 2-10. *Recent activity on your photos*

Categorizing Photos

In addition to making your photos searchable by adding titles and text, Flickr also has several ways to categorize and to group them.

Tagging Photos

Tagging is one of the most useful features that Flickr has to offer. Tagging photos is a way of categorizing photos using descriptive words. To tag a photo, click on the "Add a tag" link on the photo's page, then write the tag or tags that describe the photo. Say you want to take all the images you have of your friends, and you want to be able to look at the photos of each friend individually. You could go through each of your photos and tag them as *friend* but also tag them with the name of each individual friend in the photo. So you would have photos tagged as *dan, bill, susan,* and so on. You can also batch-tag photos as you upload them with Uploadr. Simply set the tags that you want to apply to all the photos, and every photo you upload will be tagged appropriately.

Once you've tagged your photos, retrieving them is a piece of cake. Type the following URL into a browser, replacing your user ID and whatever tag you want to look up: `http://www.flickr.com/photos/your_user_id/tags/your_tag/`. For example, `http://www.flickr.com/photos/41258641@N00/tags/beth/`.

The result will look something like Figure 2-11.

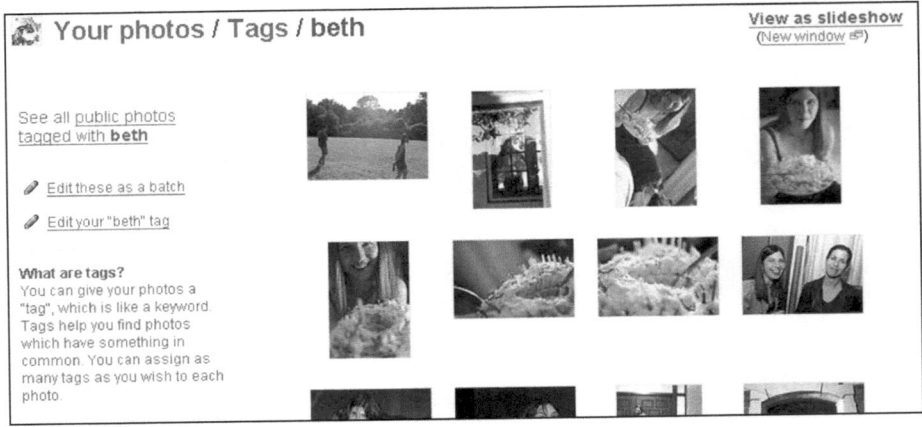

Figure 2-11. *Viewing a tag page*

You can watch a slideshow of these particular images by clicking the "View as slideshow" link in the upper right-hand corner of the page.

Note If you want to dispense with the user ID section of the URL, you can select a more meaningful path for your photos. Go to You ➤ Your Account ➤ Set up your URL. You can then, for example, assign your screen name as part of the URL instead of your user ID. So `http://www.flickr.com/photos/41258641@N00/tags/beth/` would become `http://www.flickr.com/photos/goodlux/tags/beth/`.

You can also get to your tags by clicking the You ➤ Your Tags link. This will show the top 150 of your tags on the screen in different sizes (Figure 2-12). The larger the tag, the more times you have used it.

Figure 2-12. *Top 150 tags*

An interesting feature of tags is that they can be searched globally. While each individual user has their own tags, tags also have a larger role in the group pool. Instead of looking at just your own photos, you can look at everyone's photos for a particular tag. This has some interesting results, because the same words mean different things to different people.

For instance, searching on the tag *downtown* will bring up urban images from cities all over the world. Searching on a name such as *Dave* brings up a sampling of the many faces of Dave. It's quite interesting to see what a particular word means to the world.

To search using tags, use the search box at the top of the page. Type the word you are interested in searching for and click SEARCH. An alternate way to get to the same place is by typing in the following URL, replacing tag_to_search with whatever tag you want to look up: http://www.flickr.com/photos/tags/tag_to_search/. You can also click on Explore ➤ Popular Tags. This takes you to the Tags page, where you can see the most popular tags for the past day, week, and of all time.

There are two features on an individual tag page that are noteworthy. First, if you scroll down to the bottom of the page, you will see a list of tags that are related to the tag that you searched for. So if you are looking at the tag *barcelona*, related tags are *sunset*, *graffiti*, and *roof*. There are also "see also" tags, which in the case of Barcelona are *sabatlló*, *metro*, *batllo*, *music*, *sign*, and *boqueria*. Second, on the Tags page there is the clustering feature, represented by a link on the left-hand side of the tag's page.

Clusters are groups of words that have an affinity for each other. For instance, when you tag your own photos, you might find that when you tag a photo with *birthday*, you often also tag it with *party*. The same thing happens globally. In fact, if you look at the *birthday* tag, you will see that *party*, *cake*, *friends*, *family*, *candles*, and *food* are all part of the same cluster.

Tags and clustering are extremely interesting and incredibly useful features. So much so that we've devoted a whole chapter to the subject. For more information on how you can put tags to use, take a look at Chapter 7.

Sets

In addition to tagging, another option for categorizing is to use sets. Sets allow you to group your photos by a common theme and make them easily accessible from your main photo page or from your sets page. Unlike tags, sets allow you to select a main photo to represent the whole set and to add a description for the entire set.

To create a new set, go to the main page for the photo you want to add to the set. From the icons above the photo, click the ADD TO SET icon. If you haven't created a set before, you will be asked to create a new set. If you've done this before, you can click the "create a new set" link if none of your existing sets fits the bill (Figure 2-13).

Enter a title and description for the set in the text areas that appear, and your set is created. You will notice that when you click the ADD TO SET icon in the future, your new set appears on the list. Next time you want add a photo, it's as easy as clicking the drop-down menu and picking the set.

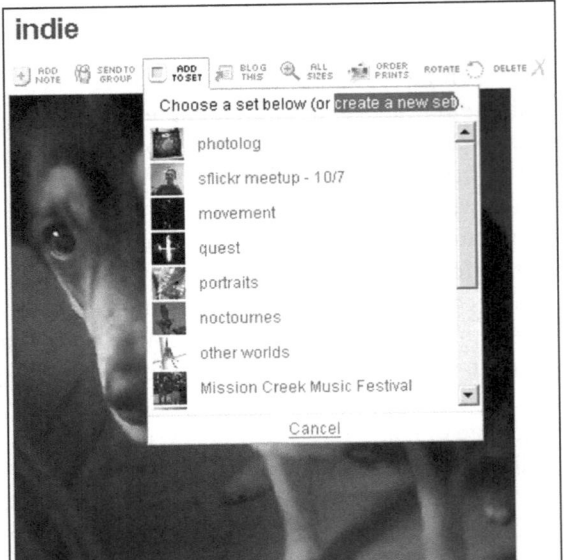

Figure 2-13. *Creating a new set*

To view your new set, go to your main page by clicking the You ➤ Your Sets link, which takes you to your sets page (Figure 2-14). Here you will see all of the sets that you've created. You have the option of editing any particular set, which allows you to easily remove photos, tag them, or change their privacy settings.

Figure 2-14. *Main set page*

Groups

Sets are really useful when categorizing your own photos, but what if you want to have a collaborative effort where you create a set of images with other people? One way to do this would be to use a special tag. For instance, if you want to gather together all of the images from a wedding, you can have all of the photographers upload their photos and use a special tag, say *janeandjoeswedding*. When you search for this tag, all of the images from the wedding will come up. The problem with this is that any Flickr user can add any tag to a photo. So it would be possible for some other user to use the same tag, and their photos would also appear in the tag search.

Groups solve this problem. They allow users to make collaborative efforts but still maintain control over the images that are added to the group. They also allow for a group discussion about whatever topics the group members care to talk about.

Flickr has existing groups for pretty much every kind of photo that you can think of. There are groups for photos of Waffle Houses, UFOs, and belly buttons. Before starting a new group, you might want to check first to be sure that there isn't already a group out there with the same kinds of images.

If you do manage to come up with a group idea that no one else has come up with, you can create your own group and invite others, and they can add their own photos to the group. The result is a collection of photos, called a pool.

Setting up a group is easy, but first you will have to decide who you want to be allowed to join the group. You have three options here. First, you can make the group private, where only the people you invite are allowed to add and view photos. This is useful when you want to share photos with your friends and family, but you don't really want to make those images public to everyone. Second, you can make the group semipublic, where anyone can view the photos, but only the people you invite can add material. This comes in handy when you want to have a lot of control over the content that is added to the group, but you want to have the photos visible to the world. Third, you can make the group completely public, where anyone can join and add images to the group, and anyone can see the images. This is the best option for projects that require input from a lot of people.

To set up your group, click on the Groups link at the top of any page. This takes you to the "Your groups" page, where you can see the groups that you administer, the groups that you belong to, and the groups that you've been invited to join. From here you can create a new group by clicking the "Create your own group" link. Next, choose who you want to be allowed to join the group. You then enter a name for the group, a description, and what you want to call the members and administrators of the group. Once complete, your group is created, and you will be taken to the administration page of the group. You can change the role names for members and administrators. For instance, if you had a group for concert photos, you might want to call the members "fans" and the administrators "security." You get the idea. You can also set the URL for the group. This is a web page that will display the group page when you visit http://www.flickr.com/groups/alias/, where alias is the custom name you choose for this URL. To see the group image pool, you can go to http://www.flickr.com/groups/alias/pool/.

Now that you've created your group, you will want to invite others. To do this, click on the Invite link from the main group page. You can invite your existing contacts or someone who has never used Flickr before by giving their email address.

Next, you'll want to put some photos in your group. This is as easy as adding a photo to a set. Go to any of your individual photo pages, then from the icons across the top of the photo click the SEND TO GROUP icon. A drop-down menu with all the groups you belong to appears. Select the group you want to add your photo to, and you're done. The photo will now appear in the group pool.

Since you created the group, you are by default an administrator of the group. As an administrator, you have some special powers that you should be aware of. In addition to being able to change the group icon and other metadata about the group, you also have control over the group privacy level. These settings allow you to control who can see the group photo pool and discussion. These sections can be made public or private at your discretion. You also have the power to "kick" users or "ban" them from the group. Kicking a user temporarily removes them from the group, and they can rejoin at any time. This is a good way to warn a user that their content or comments are not wanted. Banning a user removes a user from the group, and they cannot rejoin the group until you choose to remove the ban. This is a good tactic to use if a member of your group has repeatedly posted unwanted content to the group.

To kick a user or ban them from a group, first go to the group's main page. Click the group's name, and you will see a link that says "Administration." Now click on the Members link, and you will find the options for kicking and banning users. Use judiciously!

Using Organizr

By now you might be wondering what that conspicuous Organize link at the top of every page is. At this point we've detailed annotating, categorizing, grouping, and editing. What haven't we covered in the organization arena?

When you click the Organize link, you are taken to the Organizr application. Organizr is a Flash-based application that's built into the Flickr site. It allows you to do all of the basic organizing functions in a more user-friendly manner. The only drawback to using it is that it can be a little slower than the main Flickr website, especially if you have a slow network connection or an aging laptop.

Browsing with Organizr

When using Organizr, you are first presented with the Batch Organize window. You can now drag photos into the Batch Organize window to work with them. Alternatively, you can use the "Jump to date" link to select images from a particular time period. If you want to use the date taken instead of the date uploaded to review your photos, you can check the More options ➤ Date Taken radio button.

The photos you've selected will show up in the main Batch Organize window (Figure 2-15).

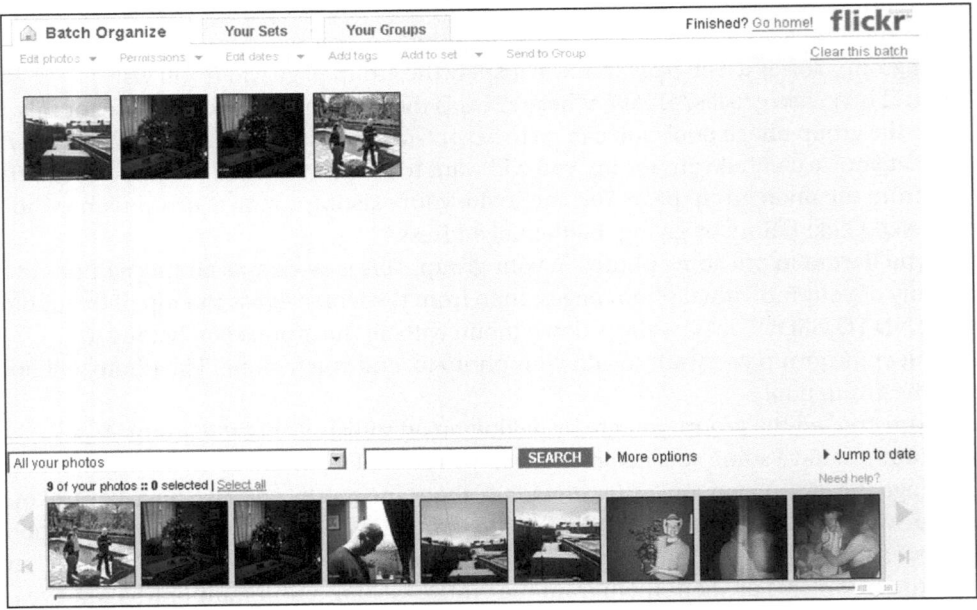

Figure 2-15. *Batch Organize window of Organizr*

When you double-click on any particular image, a new window in the Organizr will open, dedicated to just that photo (Figure 2-16).

Figure 2-16. *Individual photo page in Organizr*

This individual photo page gives you a place to change the title, description, and tags for the photo. You can also adjust the privacy settings. Remember to click SAVE to preserve any changes you've made.

Searching and Batch Operations with Organizr

You can also use Organizr to find photos. You can type in the tags or words that you want to search for in the search box at the bottom of the page. Click SEARCH, and photos matching your criteria will appear in the search window.

Notice the row of buttons at the top of the Batch Organize window. Clicking these will allow you to perform the appropriate operations on the photos that you have just retrieved: adding them to a set, adding a tag or tags to them, changing permissions on them, or even deleting them.

Working with Sets in Organizr

At the top of Organizr, you will notice there is a tab called Your Sets. If you click that tab and then double-click on one of the sets, photos from the set will start loading into the page (as shown in Figure 2-17). Double-clicking any of the photos will load the individual photo in a new window.

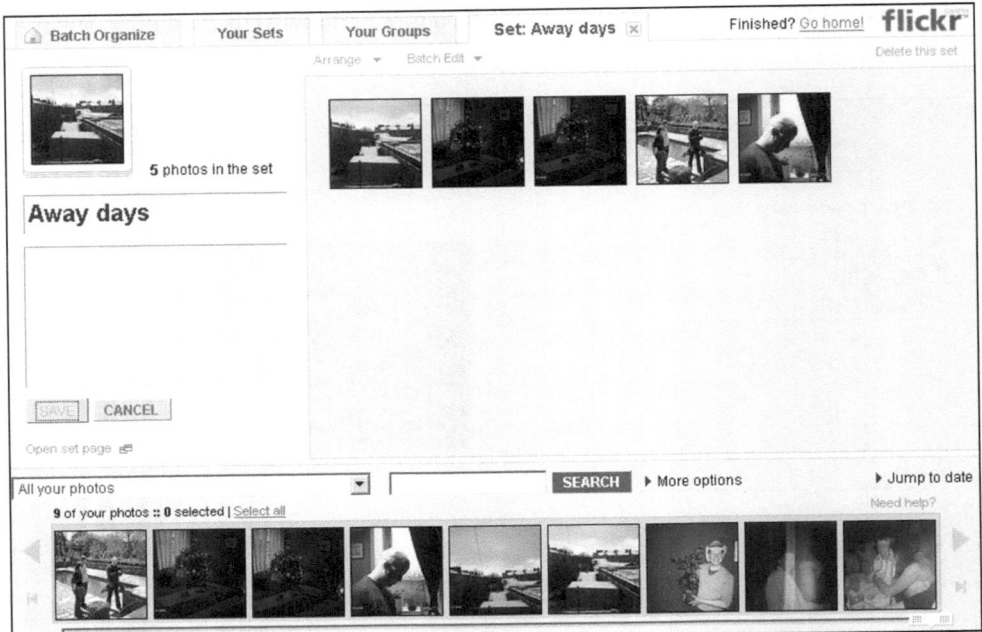

Figure 2-17. *Working with sets in Organizr*

Also, if you click a photo in the set, you'll notice that you can move the photo to a different location in the set. This will change the order of the images in the set. You can also drag an image to the lower pane of the Organizr if you want to remove it from the set, but this does not delete the image. (The photo bar will be replaced with the text "Drop a photo here to remove it from the set.") You can also drag new images from the main photo bar into the set, which is much easier than going through each photo individually.

You can also speed up adding photos to sets by holding down the **A** key (for add), and clicking the photo. This is useful when you are adding a bunch of photos to the set. Similarly, you can use the **R** key with a click to quickly remove a photo from a set. Using the Batch Edit button at the top of the set's page, you can easily add tags to all the photos in a group, change permissions of the photos, or change the date the images were taken.

Working with groups in Organizr is similar to working with sets, but there are some differences. When you click on the Your Groups tab, you will see a list of all the groups that you have permission to add images to. Click on the "Open group page" link to see thumbnails of all the images in the group. As with sets, you can drag new images into the group. However, you can remove images from the group only if you are an administrator of the group. This should be done with caution, as you could be removing someone else's photo. You can remove photos only from a group's page and not in Organizr.

Blogging with Flickr

Flickr makes a great back end for storing images for your blog. Through the Flickr web interface, it's easy to take any of the photos that you have uploaded and to post them to your blog. You'll need to do a little setup first.

Go to your account settings page by clicking the You ➤ Your Account link. From there, select the "Your blogs" link. This takes you to the administration page for your blogs (Figure 2-18). Click "Set up your blog."

Figure 2-18. *Blog administration page*

Select the type of blog you use from the drop-down menu, whether it be Blogger, Movable Type, WordPress, or one of the others. Click next and enter the API endpoint (this is the URL that Flickr uses to communicate with your blog), and your blog username and password. That's all you need to do, and you can now post directly from Flickr to your blog.

Once you've set up your blog, it's easy to add images. Go to the main photo page for the image that you want to add to the blog, then click the BLOG THIS icon just above the photo (Figure 2-19).

Figure 2-19. *Adding an image to your blog*

If you've configured more than one blog to use with Flickr, you will see each one listed on the drop-down menu. Click the blog you want to post to, then type the comments you want to show up in the entry. Click Post, and your image will appear in your blog with a reference back to the original photo page in Flickr (Figure 2-20).

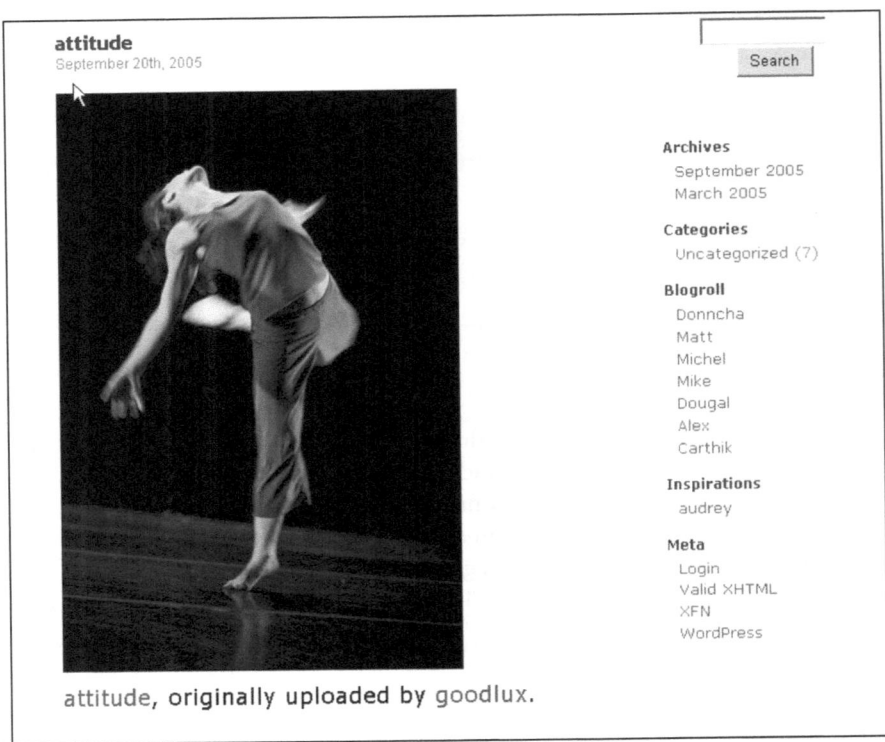

Figure 2-20. *The new image in your blog*

You can also set up Flickr to work as a moblog, or mobile blog, where images from your phone go directly to the web.

Programming with the Flickr API

In addition to all of the great features we've looked at in the chapter, there is one core functionality of Flickr that makes it stand out by far from the other photo sites on the web: it's programmable. Flickr uses an open application programming interface (API), which allows third parties to create applications that directly access the images and information stored on Flickr.

The rest of this book is dedicated to teaching you how to use PHP 5 to access Flickr. It is important to note, however, that PHP 5 is not the only language you can use to do this kind of programming. Far from it: Flickr has an API for all the popular languages, including Java, Flash ActionScript, .NET, Perl, and Python, as well as others. You can learn more about the API as well as see some of the third-party applications that have already been created at http://www.flickr.com/services/.

Summary

In this chapter we took a look at the core functionality provided through the Flickr website. We looked at uploading and editing photos, using grouping and categorization, and integrating Flickr photos into your blog. In the next chapter we will take a whirlwind tour of the PHP language as a whole. Those of you who are unfamiliar with PHP can learn to recognize features in the PHP language that will be needed to follow the examples presented later in the book.

CHAPTER 3

∎∎∎

Installing Apache, PHP, and Phlickr

In this chapter you'll learn how to install and configure the software needed to run the code recipes in this book. We'll start by showing you how to set up the software required for both Windows and Linux. This software includes the Apache web server on which you can host web pages, the PHP language, and the Phlickr library for PHP.

Even if you already have PHP installed on your computer, it's a good idea to flip through this chapter to make sure that you've got everything you need. If you're in a big hurry and think you've got everything, skip to the final verification recipes. They're designed to make sure that you've got all the required software installed and configured correctly.

Note If you are going to use the examples on your own website, you'll want to make sure that your ISP supports PHP version 5. It's a pretty major upgrade, so some ISPs haven't yet installed it. Later in the chapter we'll discuss how you can check this.

All the software is licensed under open source licenses. This means that everyone is free to download it, use it, and view the underlying source code and make any changes you might need. Because of the access to the source code, open source programs tend to get ported to many different operating systems.

Installing Apache and PHP Locally

The installation process for these software packages varies greatly depending on your operating system. It would be impossible to document the process for every operating system, so we'll focus on Windows and Linux.

Windows

Unlike most Unix vendors, Microsoft has never shipped compilers with its operating systems. As a result, most open source projects provide precompiled Windows binary files. Consequently, the Windows installation is probably the easiest.

These instructions assume that you are using Windows NT, 2000, XP, or 2003. Older versions such as Windows 95, 98, and Me will not be addressed.

You'll need to extract the files that you download in the following sections from a .zip archive. Newer versions of Windows have built-in support for ZIP files. If you're using Windows NT or 2000, you'll need a third-party program like 7-Zip (http://www.7-zip.org) or WinZip (http://www.winzip.com).

Apache

Apache is a web server that you can use to host your web pages for development on your local computer. If you're going to be using the server for production, we encourage you to consult *Pro Apache* by Peter Wainwright (ISBN 1-59059-300-6; Apress, 2004) for a more detailed discussion of how to configure and secure Apache.

Download

You'll need to download the Windows binaries from the Apache Software Foundation's website at http://httpd.apache.org/download.cgi. You'll want to select the latest revision of the Win32 binary for version 2.2. Make sure you save the file to a location on your hard drive where you can locate it.

Run the Installer

Apache comes packaged as an .msi file that uses Windows Installer to automate the installation process. Double-clicking on the file will begin the installation.

You'll be presented with the following screens that guide you through the installation process:

- **Welcome**: lets you verify the name and version of the program you're installing.

- **License Agreement**: requires you to accept the Apache License Agreement before you can continue.

- **Read This First**: gives you a chance to review the Apache HTTP Server release notes.

- **Server Information**: lets you provide a network domain, server name, administrator email address, and decide how Apache will be run. The default server and domain names detected by the installer are usually fine, but we recommend setting the administrator email address to something valid. The final setting should be set to the recommended "for All users, on Port 80, as a Service."

- **Setup Type**: allows you to choose between typical and custom setups. The typical setup installs all the required components and is recommended.

- **Destination Folder**: allows you to change the installation directory. The default directory, C:\Program Files\Apache Group\, will be used in the rest of these instructions.

- **Ready to Install the Program**: gives you a final chance to confirm the installation. After clicking Install, you can sit back and watch the blue bar. You may see several black windows pop up; this is a normal part of the installation process.

- **Completed**: simply informs you that everything has completed successfully.

After the installation process has finished, the Apache HTTP Server will be running on your local computer as a service. This means that every time your computer starts, whether you are logged in or not, the program will be running in the background.

For your convenience, a program called the Apache Service Monitor is also installed. It adds an icon to the Windows System Tray (located by default in the bottom right-hand corner of the screen by the clock). The icon allows you to tell at a glance whether the server is running or not.

Left-clicking it opens a pop-up menu allowing you to start, stop, or restart the service. Right-clicking on it opens a pop-up menu allowing you to open the server monitor form, open the Windows Services control panel (equivalent to clicking Start ➤ Control Panel ➤ Administrative Tools ➤ Services), or close down the service monitor.

Test the Apache Installation

Using your browser of choice, view http://localhost. You should see a default Apache page similar to Figure 3-1 informing you that the installation was successful.

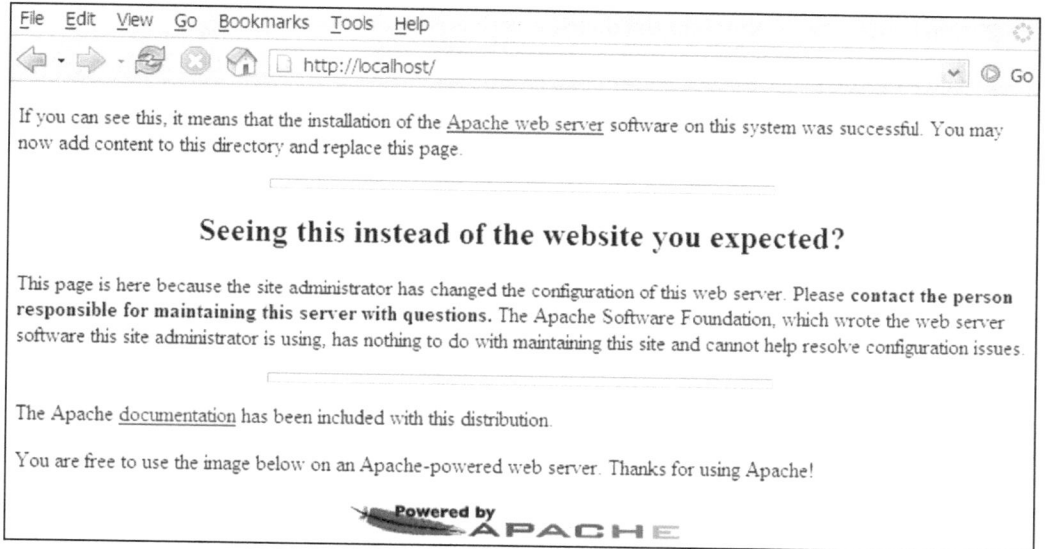

Figure 3-1. *Apache's default web page*

Note If you encounter any problems, you may want to check the official Apache Windows installation instructions at http://httpd.apache.org/docs-2.2/platform/windows.html.

PHP

As we saw in Chapter 1, PHP is an open source programming language that's frequently used to build dynamic websites. We'll use it to do so in this book, but we'll also use it from the command line to run automated scripts.

Download

Download the latest PHP 5 `.zip` file from `http://www.php.net/downloads.php`. Extract the contents of the `.zip` file to a directory named `c:\php5`.

Add PHP to the System Path

So that other programs can find PHP and its libraries, you need to add its directory to the system path.

1. In Windows Explorer, right-click on the My Computer icon. Select the Properties menu item.

2. Select the Advanced tab in the dialog box that appears.

3. Click on the Environment Variables button.

4. In the System Variables pane on the lower half of the form, locate the Path entry. (You may need to scroll to find it.)

5. Double-click on the Path entry.

6. Select the Variable Value text box and move the cursor to the end.

7. Append a semicolon and then the full path to your PHP directory; that is, `C:\WINDOWS\system32;C:\WINDOWS` becomes `C:\WINDOWS\system32;C:\WINDOWS;c:\php5`.

8. Click the OK button to save the changes.

Test the PHP Installation

To verify that PHP is in the system path and installed correctly, open a command prompt (Start ➤ Programs ➤ Accessories ➤ Command Prompt, or Start ➤ Run... and type **cmd**) and run the following command:

`C:\>php -v`

The output should be similar to the following:

```
PHP 5.1.2 (cli) (built: Jan 11 2006 16:40:00)
Copyright (c) 1997-2006 The PHP Group
Zend Engine v2.1.0, Copyright (c) 1998-2006 Zend Technologies
```

Enable Modules

PHP allows developers to extend the language by writing extensions. Most of the extensions we'll need to use are enabled by default, but we'll have to enable two additional ones: `curl` and `gd`. On Windows these are distributed as DLLs, and enabling them is as simple as uncommenting a line in the `php.ini` file.

1. Open the `php.ini` configuration file, `c:\php5\php.ini`.

2. Find the following lines and remove the leading semicolon used to comment them out.

```
;extension=php_curl.dll
;extension=php_gd2.dll
```

3. Save the file.

You can verify that the modules are enabled using the following command:

```
C:\>php -m
```

The output, with the relevant modules shown here in bold, should look like the following:

```
[PHP Modules]
bcmath
calendar
com_dotnet
ctype
```
curl
```
dom
ftp
```
gd
```
iconv
libxml
odbc
pcre
session
SimpleXML
SPL
SQLite
standard
tokenizer
wddx
xml
zlib

[Zend Modules]
```

Configure Apache

Now you'll need to configure Apache to use PHP for pages with the `.php` extension. You can open the Apache configuration file in a text editor by clicking Start ➤ Programs ➤ Apache HTTP Server 2.2.NN ➤ Configure Apache Server ➤ Edit the Apache httpd.conf Configuration File.

You'll need to add the following lines to the bottom of the file:

```
LoadModule php5_module "c:/php5/php5apache2.dll"
AddType application/x-httpd-php .php
# configure the path to php.ini
PHPIniDir "C:/php5/"
```

Test Apache and PHP

To verify that Apache is correctly configured to use the PHP module, we'll create a simple test page. Create a text file named `test.php` in Apache's document root, `C:\Program Files\ Apache Group\Apache2\htdocs`. Insert the following code:

```
<?php
phpinfo();
?>
```

With the browser of your choice, open `http://localhost/test.php`. You should see a web page with PHP's configuration information similar to that in Figure 3-2.

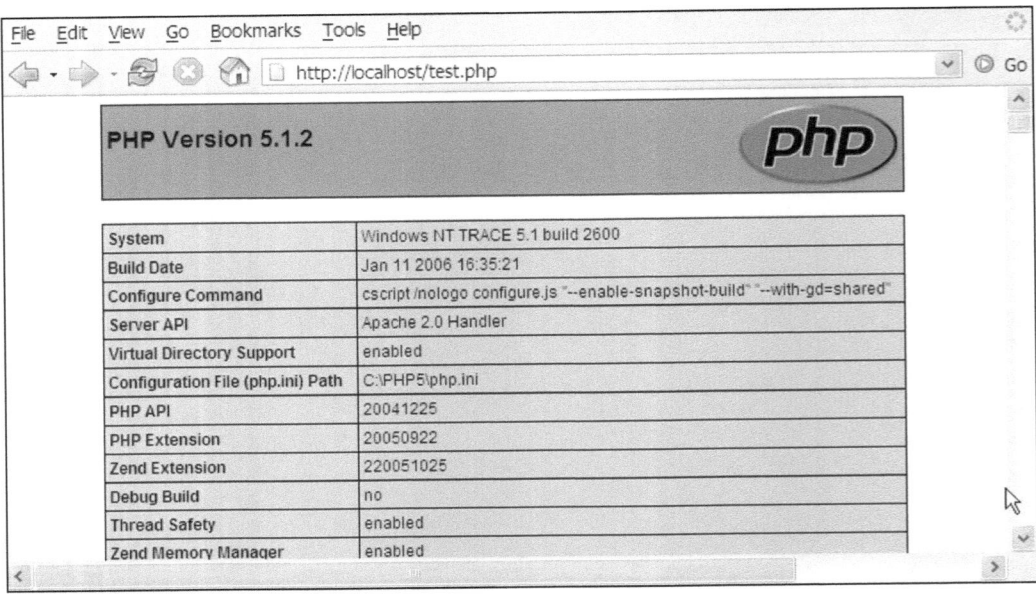

Figure 3-2. *The browser displaying the phpinfo() output confirming that Apache and PHP are installed correctly*

Note If you encounter any problems, you may want to check the official PHP Windows installation instructions at http://www.php.net/manual/en/install.windows.apache2.php.

One thing to remember is that PHP uses a list of directories called the include path to search for program files; this will become important throughout this book. The directories are searched in the order they appear in the list, first to last.

To set the include path, open the php.ini file as listed in test.php's output and edit the include_path setting:

```
;include_path=".;c:\php\includes"
```

Removing the semicolon activates the include path.

Install PEAR

The next step is to install the PEAR framework. PEAR stands for PHP Extension and Application Repository, and it's a diverse collection of PHP packages that can solve a wide variety of problems. The only feature we use in this book is the installation feature provided by the framework's core.

Open a command prompt (Start ➤ Programs ➤ Accessories ➤ Command Prompt, or Start ➤ Run... and type **cmd**). Change to the directory that PHP was installed in and then run the go-pear.bat batch file to begin the setup:

```
C:\PHP5>go-pear.bat
```

The installation process is text-based and should look something like the following:

```
Welcome to go-pear!

Go-pear will install the 'pear' command and all the files needed by
it.  This command is your tool for PEAR installation and maintenance.

Use 'php PEAR\go-pear.php local' to install a local copy of PEAR.

Go-pear also lets you download and install the PEAR packages bundled
with PHP: DB, Net_Socket, Net_SMTP, Mail, XML_Parser, PHPUnit.


If you wish to abort, press Control-C now, or press Enter to continue:
```

The PEAR developers have done an excellent job of providing logical defaults, so unless you have special configuration needs, it's safe to just keep pressing Enter until PEAR is installed.

The next step is to add the PEAR environment variables. At the command prompt, type the name of the PEAR_ENV.reg file and press Return:

```
C:\PHP5>PEAR_ENV.reg
```

Windows will recognize that this is a registry file and present a dialog box similar to the one shown in Figure 3-3, asking you to confirm that you would like to add the information to the registry. Click Yes. A second dialog box will appear informing you that the contents were successfully entered into the registry.

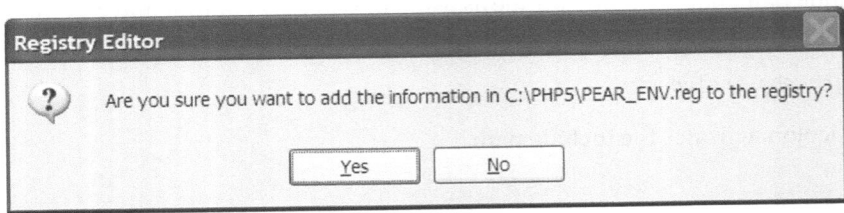

Figure 3-3. *Windows confirming that you'd like to add the PEAR settings to the registry*

The final step is to upgrade PEAR. The version released with PHP is typically a bit out of date, but PEAR can handle the upgrade itself. Run the following command to update all the installed PEAR packages:

```
C:\PHP5>pear upgrade-all
```

You'll then get a series of messages about the upgrade process that will look something like the following:

```
Will upgrade log
Will upgrade net_ftp
Will upgrade pear
Will upgrade pear_packagefilemanager
Will upgrade xml_rpc
downloading Log-1.9.3.tgz ...
Starting to download Log-1.9.3.tgz (34,792 bytes)
...done: 34,792 bytes
downloading Net_FTP-1.3.2.tgz ...
Starting to download Net_FTP-1.3.2.tgz (24,992 bytes)
...done: 24,992 bytes
downloading PEAR-1.4.9.tgz ...
Starting to download PEAR-1.4.9.tgz (283,443 bytes)
...done: 283,443 bytes
downloading PEAR_PackageFileManager-1.5.2.tgz ...
Starting to download PEAR_PackageFileManager-1.5.2.tgz (46,832 bytes)
...done: 46,832 bytes
downloading XML_RPC-1.4.5.tgz ...
Starting to download XML_RPC-1.4.5.tgz (29,172 bytes)
...done: 29,172 bytes
```

Phlickr

Phlickr is an open source PHP 5 library for accessing Flickr's web service. The majority of the examples in this book use Phlickr.

Download

Phlickr is hosted by SourceForge, the world's largest open source software development website. You can download the latest release at http://sourceforge.net/projects/phlickr/.

Install

Use PEAR to install Phlickr:

```
C:\PHP5>pear install phlickr.tgz
```

The results should be similar to the following:

```
Did not download optional dependencies: pear/PHPUnit2, use --alldeps to download
automatically
pear/Phlickr can optionally use package "pear/PHPUnit2" (version >= 2.2.0)

install ok: Phlickr
```

At this point, Apache, PHP, and Phlickr should be installed. The next step is testing everything together, so skip past the Linux installation instructions to the "Testing Phlickr" section.

Linux

These instructions discuss the process of compiling and installing the software from source code. This is not the simplest or the fastest way to accomplish the task, but it is the method that will work on the largest variety of systems.

Tip Most Linux distributions use a package manager to automate installation and upgrading of software. While a proper discussion of these tools is outside the scope of this book, it is worth noting that they are usually the best way to install PHP and Apache. The developers building the packages know the platform's quirks and how to best deal with them. You should consult the documentation for more information on exactly how to use your distribution's package manager.

For simplicity's sake, we'll make the following assumptions:

- You have root access to the machine. These instructions won't work if you're trying to install it on a machine that someone else is in charge of.

- All the software will be installed to the default location (/usr/local).

- You'll install all the software in the order listed.

The source code for these programs is usually provided in two different compressed file formats, .tar.gz and .tar.bz2. The contents are identical, but each needs a different program to uncompress them. For simplicity and to provide the widest compatibility, in these instructions we've used the .tar.gz files.

Apache

These instructions assume that you'll be using the Apache web server on your local computer only for development. If you're going to be using the server for production, we encourage you to consult *Pro Apache* by Peter Wainwright (ISBN 1-59059-300-6; Apress, 2004) for a more detailed discussion of how to configure and to secure Apache.

At the time of this writing, the current revision of Apache version 2.2 is 2.2.2, but in these instructions we'll use 2.2.x to make it clear that you need to change it.

Download

You'll need to download the source code from the Apache Software Foundation's website at http://httpd.apache.org/download.cgi. You'll want to select the latest revision of version 2.2.

Use the tar program to uncompress and extract the source code:

```
$ tar xvzf httpd-2_2_x.tar.gz
```

Change into the directory with the source code:

```
$ cd httpd-2_2_x
```

Compile and Install

Run the configure script, enabling shared modules and installing to /usr/local/apache2:

```
$ ./configure --enable-so --prefix=/usr/local/apache2
```

Use make to compile and then install Apache:

```
$ make
$ make install
```

Now that Apache is installed, start the daemon:

```
$ /usr/local/apache2/bin/apachectl start
```

Test the Apache Installation

Using your browser of choice, view http://localhost. You should see a default Apache page similar to Figure 3-4 informing you that the installation was successful.

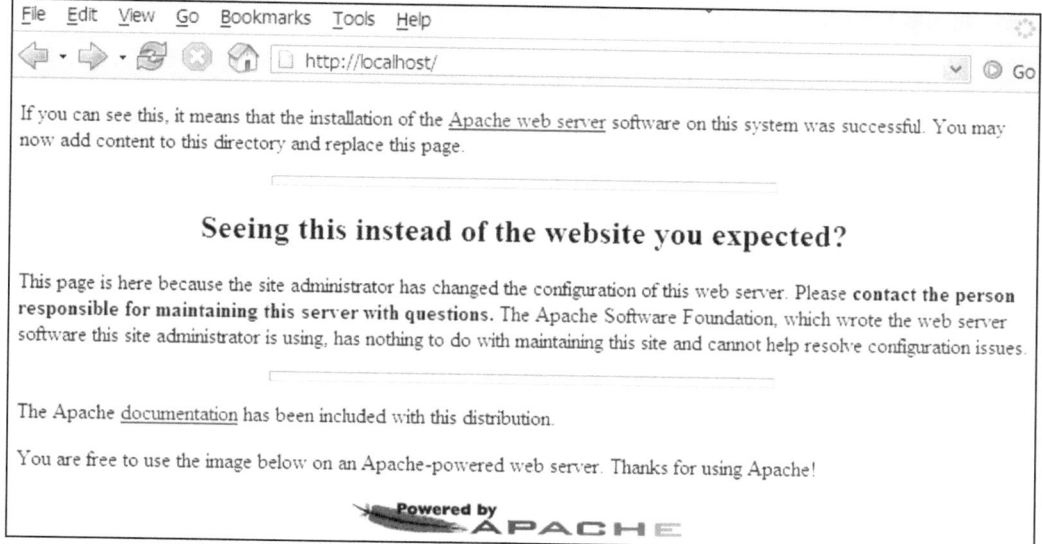

Figure 3-4. *Apache's default web page*

Note If you encounter any problems, you may want to check the official Apache installation instructions at `http://httpd.apache.org/docs-2.2/install.html`.

---

cURL

cURL is a library and command-line tool that allows you to connect and to communicate with many different types of servers using many different types of protocols.

Download

You'll need to download the source code from `http://curl.haxx.se/download.html`. Extract it using the following command:

```
$ tar xvzf curl.tar.gz
```

Change into the directory with the source code:

```
$ cd curl
```

Compile and Install

Run the `configure` script:

```
$ ./configure
```

Use make to compile and install cURL:

```
$ make
$ make install
```

Test

You can run the following command to ensure that cURL is installed correctly:

```
$ /usr/local/bin/curl http://example.com
```

The output should look something like the following:

```
<html>
<head>
  <title>Example Web Page</title>
</head>
<body>
<p>You have reached this web page by typing &quot;example.com&quot;,
  &quot;example.net&quot;, or &quot;example.org&quot; into your web browser.</p>
<p>These domain names are reserved for use in documentation and are not available
  for registration. See <a href="http://www.rfc-editor.org/rfc/rfc2606.txt">RFC
  2606</a>, Section 3.</p>
</body>
</html>
```

PHP

At the time of this writing, the current version of PHP 5 is 5.1.4, but in these instructions we'll use 5.1.x to make it clear that you need to change it.

Download

You'll need to download the source code from the PHP website at `http://www.php.net/downloads.php`. You'll want to select the latest revision of version 5.1.

```
$ tar xvzf php-5.1.x.tar.gz
```

Change into the directory with the source code:

```
$ cd ../php-5.1.x
```

Compile and Install

Configure PHP to use cURL and GD:

```
$ ./configure --with-apxs2=/usr/local/apache2/bin/apxs --with-curl=/usr/local \
 --with-gd
$ make
$ make install
```

Configure

Install the recommended PHP configuration file using the following command:

```
$ cp php.ini-recommended /usr/local/lib/php.ini
```

Test the PHP Installation

To verify that PHP installed correctly you can try the following command:

```
$ /usr/local/bin/php -v
```

The output should resemble the following:

```
PHP 5.1.2 (cli) (built: Feb 18 2006 21:23:23)
Copyright (c) 1997-2006 The PHP Group
Zend Engine v2.1.0, Copyright (c) 1998-2006 Zend Technologies
```

Upgrade PEAR

The version of PEAR released with PHP is typically a bit out of date, but PEAR is able to upgrade itself. Run the following command to update all the installed PEAR packages:

```
$ pear upgrade-all
```

You'll then get a series of messages about the upgrade process that will look something like the following:

```
Will upgrade log
Will upgrade net_ftp
Will upgrade pear
Will upgrade pear_packagefilemanager
Will upgrade xml_rpc
downloading Log-1.9.3.tgz ...
Starting to download Log-1.9.3.tgz (34,792 bytes)
...done: 34,792 bytes
downloading Net_FTP-1.3.2.tgz ...
Starting to download Net_FTP-1.3.2.tgz (24,992 bytes)
...done: 24,992 bytes
downloading PEAR-1.4.9.tgz ...
```

```
Starting to download PEAR-1.4.9.tgz (283,443 bytes)
...done: 283,443 bytes
downloading PEAR_PackageFileManager-1.5.2.tgz ...
Starting to download PEAR_PackageFileManager-1.5.2.tgz (46,832 bytes)
...done: 46,832 bytes
downloading XML_RPC-1.4.5.tgz ...
Starting to download XML_RPC-1.4.5.tgz (29,172 bytes)
...done: 29,172 bytes
```

Configure Apache

Open the Apache configuration file, typically /usr/local/apache2/conf/httpd.conf, and add the following two lines to the bottom if they do not already exist somewhere in the file.

```
LoadModule php5_module modules/libphp5.so
AddType application/x-httpd-php .php
```

Optionally, you can add the following line to use PHP files as the default page when a directory is requested:

```
DirectoryIndex index.php index.html
```

After changing the Apache configuration, you'll need to use the following command to restart the Apache server:

```
$ /usr/local/apache2/bin/apachectl start
```

Test Apache and PHP

To verify that Apache is correctly configured to use the PHP module, we'll create a simple test page. Create a text file named test.php in Apache's document root, /usr/local/httpd/htdocs. Insert the following code:

```
<?php
phpinfo();
?>
```

With the browser of your choice, open http://localhost/test.php. You should see a web page with PHP's configuration information similar to that in Figure 3-5.

■**Note** If you encounter any problems, you may want to check the official PHP installation instructions at http://us3.php.net/manual/en/install.unix.apache2.php.

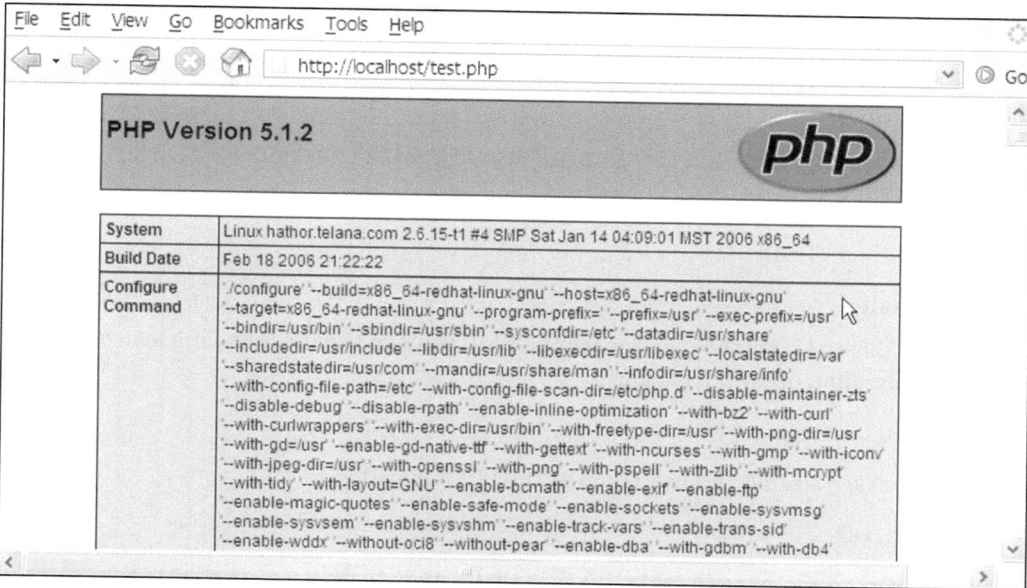

Figure 3-5. *The browser displaying the phpinfo() output confirming that Apache and PHP are installed correctly*

One thing to remember is that PHP uses a list of directories called the include path to search for program files; this will become important throughout this book. The directories are searched in the order they appear in the list, first to last.

To set the include path, open the php.ini file as listed in test.php's output and edit the include_path setting:

```
;include_path = ".:/php/includes"
```

Removing the semicolon activates the include path.

Phlickr

Phlickr is an open source PHP 5 library for accessing Flickr's web service. The majority of the examples in this book use Phlickr.

Download

Phlickr is hosted by SourceForge, the world's largest open source software development website. You can download the latest release at http://sourceforge.net/projects/phlickr.

Install Using PEAR

If you're installing Phlickr to your own machine, the easiest way is by using the PEAR installer.

```
$ pear install phlickr.tgz
```

The results should be similar to the following:

```
Did not download optional dependencies: pear/PHPUnit2, use --alldeps to download
  automatically
pear/Phlickr can optionally use package "pear/PHPUnit2" (version >= 2.2.0)
install ok: Phlickr
```

Install Manually

If you are unable to install the package using PEAR, you can use the following instructions to do it manually. First, untar the package:

```
$ tar xzf Phlickr.tgz
```

Delete the package.xml file; it's used only by the PEAR installer:

```
$ rm package.xml
```

Move the Phlickr directory to a folder that's in PHP's include path (see the include_path setting in your php.ini file):

```
$ mv Phlickr /to/some/path
```

At this point, Apache, PHP, and Phlickr should be installed. The next step is testing everything all together.

Testing Phlickr

As each piece of software was installed, you tested it individually. Now we want to test that everything works together. Create a new PHP file on the web server named phlickr_test.php. Place it in a folder called flickr at the root of your web server (C:\Program Files\Apache Group\Apache2\htdocs\flickr on Windows or /usr/local/httpd/htdocs/flickr on Linux). It should have the following contents:

```php
<?php
require_once 'Phlickr/Api.php';

define('FLICKR_API_KEY', '58ac590250ef4eeb81e6d853ee942034');
define('FLICKR_API_SECRET', '139c27ff722afe40');

$api = new Phlickr_Api(FLICKR_API_KEY, FLICKR_API_SECRET);
$response = $api->ExecuteMethod(
  'flickr.test.echo',
  array('message' => 'It worked!')
);

print "<h1>{$response->xml->message}</h1>";
?>
```

Using your browser, open the file at http://localhost/flickr/phlickr_test.php, you should see a big "It worked!" like that in Figure 3-6.

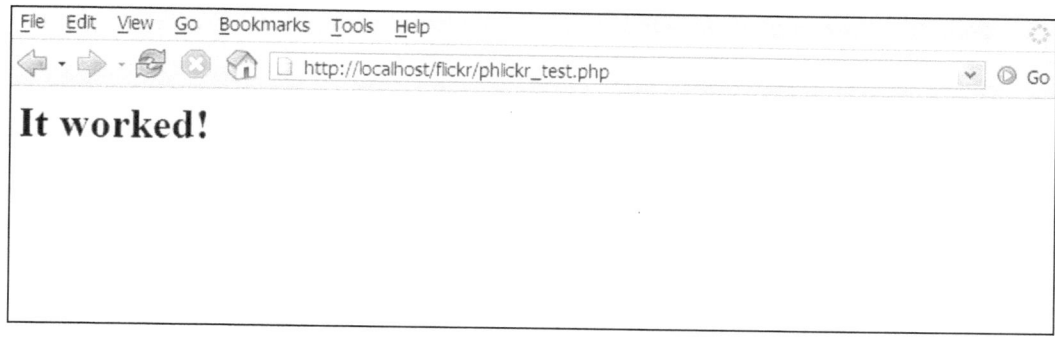

Figure 3-6. *The results of a successful run of the phlickr_test.php script*

In this case, we have sent a quick message to the Flickr website to confirm that we can talk to each other. It repeats that message back to us as confirmation.

Flickr API Keys

The final step in the setup is to obtain an API key from Flickr, which requires that each application have a unique API key. The key serves two purposes: authentication and tracking of applications. Since each application has its own key, Flickr can track the usage of applications and block applications that are abusing the service.

The primary use for the API key is user authentication. An application is uniquely identified with a key, and users can grant read, write, or delete permissions. Read permission allows the application to access all the user's photos, even those marked as private. Write permission allows all the read permissions and allows the application to add, remove, and change any of the user's photo metadata. Delete permission allows read and write permissions and allows the application to irreversibly delete the user's photos from Flickr.

The nice thing about Flickr's authentication is that a user never has to provide an application with a password. Application developers ask for permission to use the user's photos, and the user can choose to grant an application those permissions if they wish. At any point from there on, the user can revoke the permissions. This allows Flickr users more confidence that your cool application will, say, make mosaics out of their photos and won't replace all their titles with Viagra spam.

Of course, you have to assign your own application permissions to manipulate your own photos, as any other user would.

Authentication

Flickr uses a numeric value, which they call an authentication token, to link the permissions granted by a user to an application. Flickr provides different authentication methods for each of the platforms where Flickr-based applications might be used: web, desktop, and mobile. Since PHP isn't used as a programming language on mobile devices, we'll limit the discussion to desktop and web authentication.

Desktop and web authentication both follow the same basic work flow: an application requests permissions from a user, the user grants those permissions, and the application retrieves a token to act on the user's behalf. The actual specifics of the authentication process may appear overly complicated at first, but it's actually a straightforward process.

Desktop Authentication Overview

For a desktop application, the authentication steps are as follows:

1. Request a frob. A frob is a temporary, numeric value used by Flickr to identify the authentication session.

2. Build an authentication URL and direct the user to it. Your application constructs a URL that contains its API key and secret, the frob, and the desired permissions. After directing the user to this URL, you'll need them to confirm that they've granted the permissions. Then continue to the next step.

3. Convert the frob to a token. After the user has visited Flickr's website and granted your application permissions, you convert the frob into a proper authentication token. This token can then be saved so the user doesn't have to authenticate your application every time you use it.

4. Make authenticated calls. Now, your application can act as the user and, depending on the permissions, do things like search for photos, create sets, and change photo dates.

Note The term "frob" is an old bit of hacker jargon. If you're interested in reading a bit about the history of the word, check out its entry in the Jargon File at `http://www.catb.org/jargon/html/F/frob.html`.

Web Authentication Overview

Web authentication is similar to authentication for a desktop application. The main difference is that web applications don't need to request a frob. Instead, after directing the user to Flickr's site to grant permissions, Flickr will redirect the user back to a URL on your site. The URL will contain the frob, and the process continues as on the desktop. The complete steps are as follows:

1. Build an authentication URL and direct the user to it. Your application constructs a URL that contains its API key and secret, and the desired permissions. Then, you'll redirect the user to the URL.

2. Handle Flickr's authentication callback. After the user has granted your application's requested permissions, Flickr will redirect them back to a URL on your website. A frob value will be included as a parameter of the URL.

3. Convert the frob to a token. After the user has granted your application permissions and has been redirected back to your site, you convert the frob into a proper authentication token. This token can then be saved so the user doesn't have to authenticate your application every time they use it.

4. Make authenticated calls. Now your application can act as the user and, depending on the permissions, do things like search for photos, create sets, and change photo dates.

Apply for a Key

Applying for a key is a straightforward process. If you're planning on using the API for commercial purposes, you'll need to submit a more detailed application for review by the Flickr staff.

After logging into your Flickr account, browse to `http://www.flickr.com/services/api/key.gne`. Fill in your name and email address and provide a description of how you're planning to use Flickr's API (Figure 3-7). After submitting the form—assuming it's a noncommercial key request—you'll be presented with a 32-character string that is your API key.

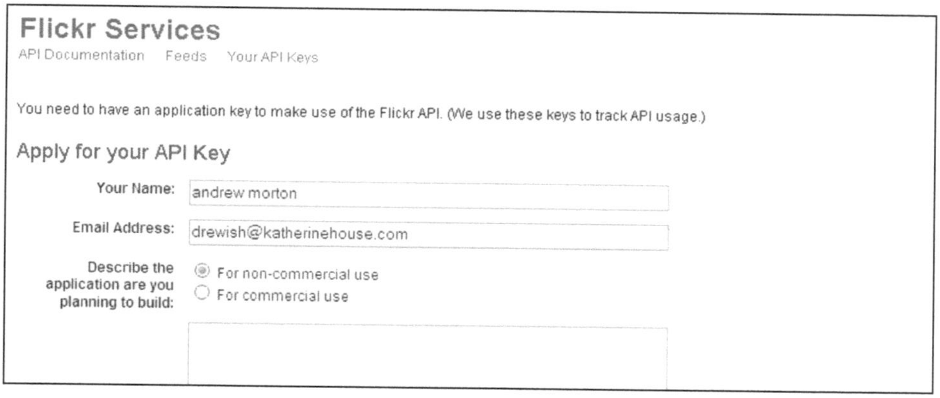

Figure 3-7. *This is the form you'll need to fill out to apply for an API key from Flickr.*

Configuring Authentication

You'll need to enable authentication for the API key you just set up by browsing to `http://www.flickr.com/services/api/keys/`.

You'll be presented with a list of keys registered to your account like that shown in Figure 3-8.

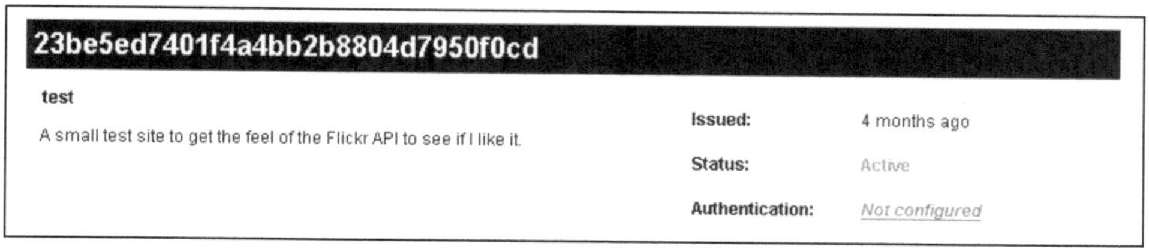

Figure 3-8. *The list of API keys on one of the author's Flickr account*

There should be a link labeled Authentication under the newly created key. Clicking that takes you to a form that lists the shared secret and has fields for you to set the title and description of your application as shown in Figure 3-9. Fill in the title and description, and then select Desktop Application as the authentication type.

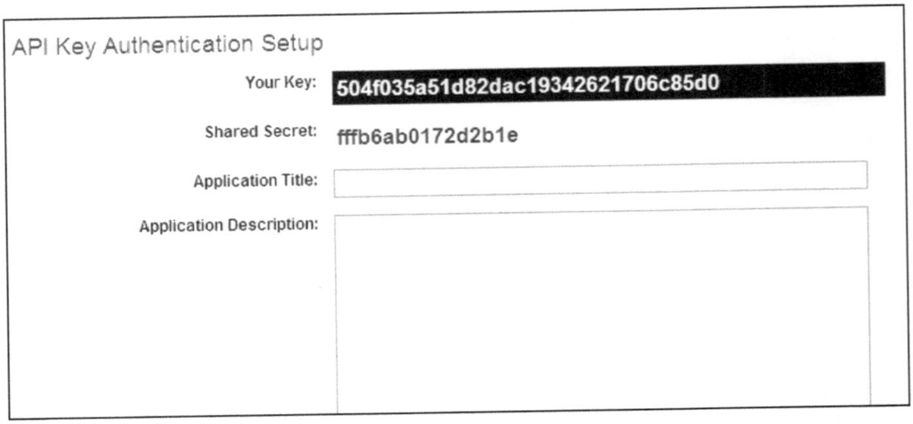

API Key Authentication Setup

Your Key: 504f035a51d82dac19342621706c85d0

Shared Secret: fffb6ab0172d2b1e

Application Title:

Application Description:

Figure 3-9. *The authentication form for an API key*

So now we have a key that can uniquely identify our application to Flickr and the user. We can use this to get authorization from a user to work with their photos.

Later on you may want to use web authentication, but for now we'll use desktop authorization so we can walk through the process of obtaining an authorization token.

Getting an Authorization Token

To use the samples in this book, you'll want to get an authorization token of your own for testing. To do this you'll need the API key and secret you obtained in the previous two sections.

Note This section requires a bit of prior PHP knowledge to fully understand. If you find yourself confused by it, skip ahead to the next chapter, brush up on PHP, and then come back and finish the process of obtaining an authorization token.

The following PHP program will use the Phlickr library to step through the authentication process and obtain a token. You should have already completed the Phlickr setup on your local computer. Create a new text file, enter the contents, and then save the file as get_token.php.

```php
<?php
include_once 'Phlickr/Api.php';

// Prevent from enforcing a time limit on this script
set_time_limit(0);

print "This script will help you retrieve a Flickr authorization token.\n\n";
```

```php
// Get the user's API key and secret.
print 'API Key: ';
$api_key = trim(fgets(STDIN));
print 'API Secret: ';
$api_secret = trim(fgets(STDIN));

// Create an API object, then request a frob.
$api = new Phlickr_Api($api_key, $api_secret);
$frob = $api->requestFrob();
print "Got a frob: $frob\n";

// Find out the desired permissions.
print 'Permissions (read, write, or delete): ';
$perms = trim(fgets(STDIN));

// Build the authentication URL.
$url = $api->buildAuthUrl($perms, $frob);
print "\nOpen the following URL and authorize:\n$url\n";
print "\nPress Return when you're finished...\n";
fgets(STDIN);

// After they've granted permission, convert the frob to a token.
$token = $api->setAuthTokenFromFrob($frob);

// Print out the token.
print "Auth token: $token\n";
?>
```

We will run this script at the command line. To do so, we will use the php executable to parse the file and run the code without going through the Apache web server. If we were to use Apache, it would take our request for the script, use PHP, and then return the results. Here we skip the middleman.

To run the script, open up a command prompt or terminal (depending on your operating system), change to the directory where you saved the file, and run the following command:

```
> php get_token.php
```

Running the script should produce output resembling the following:

```
This script will help you retrieve a Flickr authorization token.

API Key: 58ac590250ef4eeb81e6d853ee942034
API Secret: 139c27ff722afe40

Got a frob: 1292322-495524f7be669367
Permissions (read, write, or delete): write
```

```
Open the following URL and authorize:
http://flickr.com/services/auth/?api_key=58ac590250ef4eeb81e6d853ee942034&frob=12923
22-495524f7be669367&perms=write&api_sig=7c6419d04e32edc662e91065b17fdd83

Press Return when you're finished...

Auth token: 418262-6b5d298dcffcf131
```

The program will interactively prompt you for your API key and secret, then the permissions you'd like to grant the application. It will output a very long URL that you'll need to paste into your browser. The resulting web page will display the application's title and description and confirm that you want to grant the requested permissions. Confirming this will result in a success message similar to that in Figure 3-10.

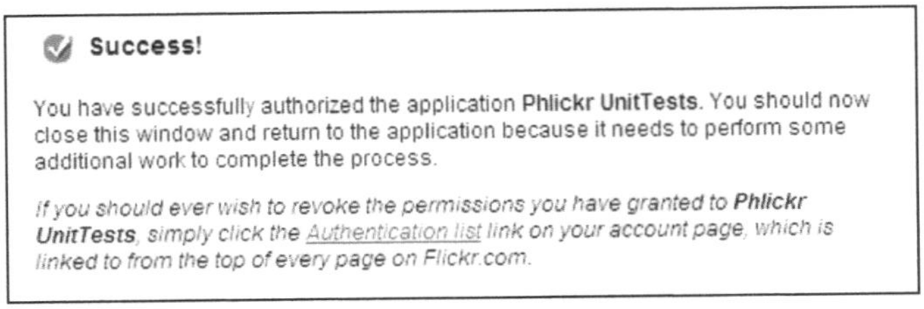

> ✅ **Success!**
>
> You have successfully authorized the application **Phlickr UnitTests**. You should now close this window and return to the application because it needs to perform some additional work to complete the process.
>
> *If you should ever wish to revoke the permissions you have granted to **Phlickr UnitTests**, simply click the Authentication list link on your account page, which is linked to from the top of every page on Flickr.com.*

Figure 3-10. *This is the confirmation Flickr displays after you've authorized an application.*

Now, return to the waiting get_token.php script and press Return. The script will print out the value of the authorization token.

We'll use the following file format in this book when working with Flickr:

```
api_key=58ac590250ef4eeb81e6d853ee942034
api_secret=139c27ff722afe40
api_token=418262-6b5d298dcffcf131
```

Save this as a file called authtoken.dat, making sure that it contains your values as appropriate.

Checking Your ISP's Setup

If you're going to be using the code samples from this book on your ISP's web server, most of the setup has already been done for you. In this section we'll just verify that everything is set up and working correctly.

PHP

The first thing to check is that the correct version of PHP is installed. Phlickr, the package we use to connect to Flickr's API, requires PHP 5. To check the version, we'll create a simple test page that will display PHP's configuration information.

Begin by creating a text file named php_test.php with the following contents:

```
<html>
  <head>
    <title>PHP Tests</title>
  </head>
  <body>
    <h1>PHP Version <?php print phpversion(); ?></h1>
    <p>Include path: <?php print get_include_path(); ?></p>
    <p>Installed extensions:</p>
    <ul>
      <li><?php print implode('</li><li>', get_loaded_extensions()); ?></li>
    </ul>
  </body>
</html>
```

Assuming that one doesn't already exist, create a new directory on your web server named flickr and upload the file to it. If a directory of that name does exist, call the new one flickr2, and use that name instead for the rest of these instructions. The exact details of how to create a directory and upload files depend on your ISP, so if you haven't done it before and don't feel comfortable, contact the tech support staff.

Once you've uploaded the file to your web server, use a browser to open it. If the root of your website is http://example.com and you used the recommended directory and file names, then the URL would be http://example.com/flickr/php_test.php. The output should look something like Figure 3-11.

Figure 3-11. *The test page output displaying PHP's version, include path, and installed modules*

The first thing you'll want to check is that the version listed at the top is PHP 5.0.0 or greater. Anything less than that is unsupported by Phlickr. The next thing you'll want to do is scroll down and make sure that gd and SimpleXML are listed as installed extensions. If both are installed and PHP is version 5 or greater, then you're in good shape. If not, you'll need to contact your ISP to ask about either installing the extensions, upgrading PHP, or both.

Determining the Include Path

Looking at Figure 3-11, you may have noticed a line labeled "Include path." This information will help you when trying to determine where to install Phlickr. You'll either need to place the files into one of these directories that's already in the include path or, if you install it somewhere else, add the directory to the include path.

To help make sense of the include path, let's look at an example from one of our websites:

```
.:/www/amorton/include:/usr/local/share/pear:/usr/local/lib/php/pear
```

Since the web server is a Unix machine, the colon character is used to delimit the list of directories. If this was a Windows machine, the semicolon would be used. So you don't have to worry about what operating system you're using; PHP defines a constant named PATH_SEPARATOR with the value set to the appropriate delimiter.

The first entry in the list is a single period, representing the current directory. This means that the first thing searched will be the directory where the PHP script is located. The second is a directory that the ISP provides for PHP files we want to include but that cannot be called directly from the web server, making them private as far as the outside world is concerned. The last two entries reference the PEAR libraries installed on the web server.

By doing a bit of poking around, it should become obvious which of the directories in the include path—besides the current dot directory—you can save to. If you have a writable directory, you'll be able to simply upload the Phlickr directory into it and be on your way. If you don't have any writable directories, you'll need to create a new directory and add it to the include path. In the next section we discuss how to go about doing that.

Note This section requires a bit of prior PHP knowledge to fully understand. If you find yourself confused by it, skip ahead to the next chapter, brush up on PHP, and then come back and finish the setup on your ISP's web server.

Adding Directories to the Include Path

If you determine that you need to add a directory to the include path, there are a couple of ways to do it. Each method has its advantages and drawbacks.

Using set_include_path()

The simplest way to change the include path is to add code to the top of each PHP program to load the current include path and add your directories to it. If you have only a single page or two, this will probably be the best approach. The downside is that if you decide to add a directory, you'll have to modify all your pages to add it.

You can use the following code to display the current include path, then to add a directory named /www/includes, and then to print out the new include path:

```php
<?php
print get_include_path() ."\n";
$path = '/www/includes';
set_include_path(get_include_path() . PATH_SEPARATOR . $path);
print get_include_path();
?>
```

The boldface lines show how to retrieve the include path and to concatenate it with the correct platform-specific path separator and then the new directory.

Using an .htaccess File

Assuming that your ISP uses Apache, a slightly more complex but far more useful method is to set the include path in an .htaccess file. Apache uses files named .htaccess to allow configuration changes on a per-directory basis. You can override PHP's include path by adding the following Apache directive:

```
php_value include_path ".:/www/amorton/include:/www/includes"
```

If there's no existing file named .htaccess you can create a new text file with that name and add the line to it. If the file exists, check and see whether it's already setting the include path. If so, just add your directory to the end of the directive. If it's not setting the include path, add the directive to the end of the file.

There are a few things to keep in mind with this approach.

- This approach overwrites the existing path. If we used it to change the example include path used earlier, we would no longer have access to the PEAR libraries. If you want to preserve the existing directories, you'll need to add those by hand.

- The include path will apply to all the PHP files in the current directory and all subdirectories. On Apache, unless a subdirectory overrides the settings, options in one .htaccess file apply to that directory and all its children.

- Since this isn't PHP code, you can't use the PATH_SEPARATOR constant. If your ISP is using Apache on Windows, you'll need to use semicolons to separate the paths.

Note If you find that you are unable to set the include path from the .htaccess file, contact your ISP's tech support staff and verify that the AllowOverride Options or AllowOverride All directive is set on your directory or virtual host.

Installing Phlickr

Now that you've verified the setup of PHP on your ISP's server and determined a location in the include path where you can install Phlickr, it's time to get to it. The process will vary depending on how your ISP allows you to access their server. The basic idea is that if you have a directory named includes, you'll want to end up with a subdirectory named Phlickr with Api.php and the other files in it as shown in the following code:

```
includes/
  Phlickr/
    Framework/
    Import/
    [...]
    Api.php
    AuthedGroup.php
    [...]
    User.php
    UserList.php
```

Shell Access

If your ISP allows you shell access via Telnet or SSH (secure shell) and you're comfortable using Unix commands, the easiest thing would be to use the instructions in the preceding "Linux" section under "Install Manually." In most cases you'll find that, due to security restrictions, you won't be able to use the PEAR installer and will need to use the manual instructions.

FTP or SCP Access

If your ISP allows you to upload files only via FTP or SCP, the easiest way to install Phlickr is to download the package to your computer, extract it, and then upload the uncompressed files.

Summary

In this chapter we've walked you through the steps you'll need to install PHP, an Apache web server, and the Phlickr package on your own computer. We went through the process of obtaining a Flickr API key and authorization token. Finally, we went through the steps to verify that you'll be able to use the Phlickr package on your ISP's web server. At this point you should be all set to try out any of the examples in this book. In the next chapter we'll connect to Flickr's web service and start having some fun.

CHAPTER 4

■ ■ ■

PHP Basics for Flickr

In order to get the most out of this book, you will need to be able to recognize some basic features of the PHP language. In this chapter, we will point out the basics of PHP that you will need to familiarize yourself with, so you can follow the rest of the examples in this book. That said, this is only an extremely quick gloss over the essential features of the language. If you want to learn the language in more detail, we recommend that you take a look at the official PHP website (http://www.php.net). As a newcomer, you'll really appreciate how well the language is documented. For further reference and careful tutorials, we recommend *Beginning PHP and MySQL 5: From Novice to Professional* by W. Jason Gilmore (ISBN 1-59059-552-1; Apress, 2006).

If you've already had a good deal of experience with PHP, you can safely skip over this chapter and go right to Chapter 5, where we begin working with the Flickr API. If you are already a programmer but haven't used PHP, skimming this chapter may fill in some gaps for you. Finally, if you are a complete newbie to programming, this chapter was written with you in mind. You should find this chapter worth the time it takes to read. By the time you've completed this chapter, you should be able to read through a block of PHP code, identify the basic language components in the code, and have some understanding of what the code does.

Overview of PHP

In order to really understand the value of PHP, it's helpful to understand a little bit about web pages generally. Web pages are written in a language called HTML, which provides a standardized means of structuring and formatting a web page. The files contain the text that will be displayed as well as additional information called *tags*, which tell the web browser how to display the content. The page is stored in text files named with an .htm or .html extension to tell the web server that it is an HTML file.

```
<html>
  <head>
    <title>A simple HTML page</title>
  </head>
  <body>
    <h1>This is big text.</h1>
    <h3>This is smaller text.</h3>
  </body>
</html>
```

By itself, HTML is great for static web pages where the information in the page changes rarely, if ever. While it may be informative, a static HTML website is rather limited in what it can do. It is unable to accept a user's input, display information from a database, or change appearance based on the user—a few of the more common features that users have come to expect from a website. For instance, Flickr's site is constantly changing, with an endless stream of new photos appearing all the time.

This is where scripting languages like PHP come in handy. They make it easy for a programmer to build dynamic web pages that change frequently and have much more functionality than just displaying static information in a browser.

Note To use the rest of the examples in this chapter you'll need to have access to a web server running PHP. Instructions for setting up PHP and the Apache web server on your computer can be found in Chapter 3.

You can easily recognize PHP code, because it almost always begins with the tag `<?php` and ends with `?>`. These are called the opening tag and closing tag, respectively. PHP scripts are stored in text files with a `.php` extension. A very basic PHP program looks like this:

```php
<?php
echo "I'm PHP code!";
?>
```

Saving this to a file on your web server, making sure that the file name has the `.php` extension, and pointing your browser at its URL (for example `http://localhost/examples/first.php`) will produce the following output:

```
I'm PHP code!
```

Here we are using the PHP echo command to display some text. This command simply parrots to the web server anything that follows it. The web server processes this and sends it out to the browser, which displays the text.

Notice also the semicolon at the end of the line. Every statement in PHP ends with a semicolon. This allows the PHP engine to separate one instruction from the next. A forgotten semicolon will likely be the source of many of the errors in the code you write.

In the preceding example, we weren't using HTML; our script just returned unformatted text. Next we will take the preceding example and embed it into HTML.

```html
<html>
  <head>
    <title>PHP test</title>
  </head>
  <body>
```

```
  <h1>
    <?php
    echo "I'm PHP code!";
    ?>
  </h1>
 </body>
</html>
```

```
I'm PHP code!
```

In your browser, you will see the same text, but this time it will be bigger and bolder. This is because the text is surrounded by HTML <h1> (Heading 1) tags, which instruct the browser to make the text very large and bold.

Here's how it works. First the web browser (the client) requests a page from the web server. The web server goes and gets the page and finds it has a .php extension. So the web server hands off the page to the PHP engine and waits for PHP to respond. The PHP engine then processes the code, leaving the HTML as it is, and gives the results of this processing back to the web server. In this case, the result was simply the string "I'm PHP code!" Finally, the web server hands the processed page to the web browser.

The important thing to note here is that all of the processing happens on the server. This is called *server-side scripting*. The client browser never actually sees any PHP code itself; it sees only the results of that code being run. One great thing about this is that the code is somewhat private. Since the browser never actually sees the code, you could, for instance, have the secret password to your database included in the code. If the code were running on the client, someone could easily read the password.

Another reason server-side scripting is useful is that as long as the output of the script adheres to standards, any browser that supports those standards can read it. So you shouldn't have to write different code for different browsers, and you don't have to worry about whether or not the browser can run the code.

PHP Comments

Another basic feature of a PHP program that you will definitely need to be able to recognize are comments. These are just notes that the author of the code wanted to jot down but that have no bearing on execution of the code. Comments are also used to disable code without deleting it from the file when you are debugging a program. There are two types of comments in PHP: either a multiline comment or a single-line comment. Both are demonstrated in the following example.

```
<?php
/*
This is a multiline comment. Everything until the closing symbol will be ignored
echo "This statement won't show up because it is commented out.";
*/
```

```
// This is a single-line comment

# This is also a single-line comment

echo "This is part of the results.\r\n"; // Comments can be after code...
echo "This text will show up.\r\n";       # ...using either single-line format
?>
```

If you run the preceding code at the command line, you will get the following:

```
This is part of the results.
This text will show up.
```

As you can see in the preceding example, multiline or block comments are surrounded by the begin comment symbol (/*) and the end comment symbol (*/). If you just want to comment out a single line, you can use either the double slash (//) or the pound sign (sometimes called hash) symbol (#). These symbols comment out everything that follows them until the end of the line. They do not affect the code that comes before them, as shown in the preceding example.

The \r\n string is the carriage return character (\r) followed by the newline character (\n), which essentially says to end the current line and start a new one. (On Linux you need only the newline character, but we're catering for all users here, and Windows needs the carriage return.) This is used so all of the output is not crammed together on one line.

PHP Variables

Now that we know what a very basic piece of PHP code looks like, we can explore some ways to fill up the space between the question mark brackets. Let's begin with variables.

Variables are the workhorses of any programming language. They tote around all the information like abstract dump trucks, carrying information throughout your programs. For our purposes in this book, variables will be used to hold the titles and identifiers of photos, photo sets, and groups, as well as many other things.

If you are completely new to programming it might be helpful to think of a variable as a box that information can be stored in. The box has its name written on the outside, and when you want to use the information that is in the box, you use the box's name to refer to the contents.

You can recognize variables in PHP code by looking for the dollar sign ($). As a rule, all variables in PHP must begin with the dollar sign $ and be followed by either a letter or underscore. Aside from that, you can be pretty creative; the variable can then have any number of letters, numbers, or underscores after the initial character. So the following are acceptable (but not very useful) variable names:

```
$____phone_number
$_01Name
$AnythingGoes
```

The following are not acceptable variable names:

```
$01Name
$#_EmployeeName
$Name&Address
```

Let's look at why these won't work. The variable $01Name starts with a number, so it's not acceptable. Similarly, $#_EmployeeName doesn't work because a PHP variable must start with an underscore or a letter. $Name&Address doesn't work, because you must have only letters, numbers, or underscores after the initial character.

One very important thing to note is that PHP variables are case sensitive. So $DumpTruck is a different variable than $dumptruck. Great care should be taken when naming variables so that you can avoid confusion later. Generally you want to keep the names short but descriptive, and you want to adhere to some sort of naming policy. For instance, you might want to say that all variables use lowercase letters only. The following are examples of well-named variables:

```
$photo_title
$group_name
$photoset_id
```

Note that all of the preceding names stick to lowercase and use an underscore to separate words for readability. The names are meaningful but not terribly excessive in length. This is the general convention we will be using throughout the book.

Now that we know what a variable looks like, we can start using them. The first thing you will want to do is to put something into a variable, or in other words *assign* a value to the variable. One way to do this is by using the assignment operator, which is the equals sign (=).

```php
<?php
$photo_title = 'Whoops!';
$photo_id = 2213133;
$photo_description = 'This is me falling down the stairs at my graduation.';

echo $photo_title . "\r\n";
echo $photo_id . "\r\n";
echo $photo_description . "\r\n";
?>
```

When run from the command line, you get the following:

```
Whoops!
2213133
This is me falling down the stairs at my graduation.
```

In the preceding example, we assigned values to variables and used the echo command to output the value stored in each variable. Notice in the echo commands the period (.) and the text that follows it. In PHP the period is the concatenation operator. It is used to combine two things. Whatever is to the left of the operator will be combined with whatever follows to the right. In this case, we are combining the value of a variable with the "\r\n" string.

PHP Data Types

In the last example, we took a quick look at the integer and string data types. *Data types* are the distinct kinds of data that can be stored in a variable. There are six data types that we are going to need to know about to cover everything in this book. They are

- String

- Boolean

- Integer

- Float

- Array

- Object

PHP has many functions for using, converting, and manipulating the different kinds of data. Our goal here is to give you the ability to recognize these data types when you come across them and to have a basic understanding of what each type is used for.

Strings

For the most part, strings are pretty straightforward. They are usually a piece of text or a word or some kind of identifier, like a Social Security number. You can recognize a string because it is enclosed in either single quotes (') or double quotes ("). The single quotes indicate that the PHP engine should process the string exactly as it is. In other words, they indicate a *literal* string. This is the most basic kind of string.

There are times, however, where simple strings are not enough. Suppose you want to insert a line break, or you want to include the value stored in a variable inside of your string. This is where the double quotes are used. The double quotes indicate to the PHP engine that it needs to take a close look inside of the quotes for variables and *escaped characters*. Some examples will help illustrate this. First let's look at simple strings.

```php
<?php
echo 'This is a simple string.';
echo 'Im also simple.';
?>
```

Running the preceding code will produce the following results, exactly as shown:

```
This is a simple string.Im also simple.
```

In the preceding example we have two simple strings enclosed in single quotes. As expected, they print exactly as specified. Notice that there is no line break in the results; everything is crammed onto one line, and there is no apostrophe in `Im`, which should be `I'm`. If we try to fix this by inserting an apostrophe, we get a parse error as in the following:

```php
<?php
echo 'This is a simple string.';
echo 'I'm also simple.';
?>
```

Parse error: parse error, unexpected T_STRING, expecting ',' or ';' in
/usr/www/users/otg/test.php on line **5**

So in order to get the results we want, we need to do two things. First, we need to add a newline character to the end of the first string, in order to have two lines. To use the newline character or other special characters, you must use double quotes. Second, we need to *escape* the apostrophe using the forward slash character (\). This instructs the engine to treat the character that follows as a literal, not as a closing quote. You can get away with single quotes in this case.

```php
<?php
echo "This is a simple string.\r\n";
echo "I\'m also simple.";
?>
```

Our new and improved results look like the following:

```
This is a simple string.
I'm also simple.
```

Finally, here's how to include a variable in the string:

```php
<?php
$count = 2;
echo "There are $count photos in this set.";
?>
```

This produces the following:

```
There are 2 photos in this set.
```

The $count variable is filled in by PHP when it is included in double quotes.

If this seems a little confusing, don't be alarmed; it really *is* confusing. The important things to remember here are the following:

- You can identify strings in PHP code because they are surrounded by quotation marks.

- Sometimes strings have to be specially formatted, so the information between the quotation marks may sometimes include special characters that don't actually show up in the output when the code is run.

With this in mind, let's take a look at the next data type, Boolean.

Boolean

While the string data type allows us to store a myriad of different values, the Boolean data type is much more limited. It can hold only one of two values: TRUE or FALSE.

Boolean data is useful for controlling the flow of a program. It is often combined with programmatic control structures, which we will discuss in greater detail a little further on in this chapter. Together, they are used to check on the state of things and make a decision based on the results. To illustrate this, we will look at a simple example that uses the if...else control structure. We will describe control structures in greater detail later in the chapter, but for now you can just think of the if...else structure as a way for the code to decide which statements to execute.

```php
<?php
$photo_uploaded = TRUE;

if ($photo_uploaded) {
  echo "The photo has been uploaded.";
} else {
  echo "The photo has not been uploaded.";
}
?>
```

When we run this code, we get the following results:

```
The photo has been uploaded.
```

In the previous example, we assigned the Boolean value TRUE to the variable $photo_uploaded. The if statement is then used to check the value of $photo_uploaded. If the value is TRUE, then the program responds by outputting that the photo has indeed been uploaded. If the value is FALSE, it outputs that the photo has not been uploaded.

Integer

The integer data type is useful when you want to count or enumerate something. It is used to store whole numbers, both negative and positive. You can locate integers in PHP code by looking for numbers that do not have a decimal point and are not surrounded by quotation marks. The following are all examples of variables that have been assigned integer data.

```php
<?php
$photo_id = 199924;
$count = 0;
$total = -4;
?>
```

Float

Like integers, the float data type is used to store numbers. These numbers, however, are floating-point decimal numbers, suitable for precise results. When you use code that performs calculations, it is very likely that the data is stored as floating-point number. You can recognize float data in PHP code as any number that has a decimal point. Sometimes floating-point numbers will be expressed with scientific notation, using the e or E symbol to express the exponent. The following are examples of variables that have been assigned float data:

```php
<?php
$average = 2.34;
$bignumber = 1.54e15;
$smallnumber = 2.34E-20;

echo $average."<br/>";
echo $bignumber."<br/>";
echo $smallnumber."<br/>";
?>
```

This time we are catering for the web audience by adding a break tag. Following are the results if viewed in a browser:

```
2.34
1.54E+15
2.34E-20
```

> **Note** These first four data types are scalar, meaning they store a single quantity or value. The remaining two types that we will be discussing are compound data types that use combinations of scalar data.

Array

The array data type stores an ordered data map. This map is made up of a list of values and a corresponding key for each value. Each key is unique, so when you want to get the value later, you just specify the key. Arrays are extremely flexible and can be put to use in a limitless number of tasks.

To create an array, you use the array() construct. Assigning an array to a variable looks like the following:

```php
$photo_id_list = array ( 1 => '9756830', 2 => '22567557', 3 => '22567560');
```

Here we've assigned the value "9756830" to the key 1, the value "22567557" to the key 2, etc. If we want to get those values out of the array later, we specify the variable name and the key that corresponds to the value that we want to retrieve. Consider the following code:

```php
<?php
$photo_id_list = array ( 1 => '09756830', 2 => '22567557', 3 => '22567560');
echo $photo_id_list [2]."<br/>";
echo $photo_id_list [1]."<br/>";
echo $photo_id_list [3]."<br/>";
?>
```

It outputs the following when run:

```
22567557
09756830
22567560
```

If you are creating an array that uses incremental integer values (1, 2, 3, 4, etc.) for keys as we have done in the preceding example, there is a shortcut you can use when creating your array. If you just use the array construct without specifying keys, the PHP engine will automatically assign keys for you, though the keys begin at 0. Here's an example:

```php
<?php
$photo_titles = array ('kind of blue', 'fabulous meek', 'smashed');
echo $photo_titles[1];
?>
```

This returns the following results, because 1 is the second key:

```
fabulous meek
```

You're not constrained to using only integer values for keys. If you like, you can use strings as well, as long as they are unique.

```php
<?php
$photo_list = array ('song6830' => 'fabulous meek' ➥
        'song7224' => 'kind of blue', ➥
        'song6322' => 'smashed');
echo $photo_titles['song7224'];
?>
```

Following is the result:

```
kind of blue
```

Notice that when we retrieve the value in the echo statement, the key is surrounded with quotes, because the key is string data, rather than an integer.

Object

The final data type that we will be taking a look at is the object data type. In order to fully understand objects and how they function, you will really need to read up on object-oriented programming concepts. For our purposes, though, it is enough to know that objects are complex programmatic structures used in creating software models. Objects are abstract "things" that have attributes or properties like name, color, weight, and size. They also are capable of performing actions or functions. For instance, they can blink into existence, move around, or disappear. Exactly what they are and what they are capable of is limited only by the imagination of the programmer who designs them.

Given that objects can be just about anything, you would think that they might be difficult to identify, but recognizing an object in PHP code is quite easy. Objects are called into existence, or *instantiated*, using the new keyword, so you can spot objects when they are being created. Objects can be created anywhere in a block of code, but often they are created early on, somewhere near beginning of the code. For example, see the following:

```php
<?php
// In practice, Photo class would be defined here

$p = new Photo();

$p->id = '5859628';
$p->title = 'This is a test photo';
$p->URL = 'http://photos3.flickr.com/5859628_64c58f62a3.jpg';
$p->savePhoto();

echo $p->id."<br/>";
echo $p->title."<br/>";
echo $p->URL."<br/>";
?>
```

In the preceding example, we have created an object, $p, which is a Photo object. Since all Photo objects have certain properties, we can assign $p certain values. In this case, we give $p an ID, a title, and a URL so we can look it up on the web. After setting these few properties of the object, we then save $p using the savePhoto() method, which is part of our hypothetical Photo object. Then we output the properties to the browser using echo. Keep in mind that this is just an example for illustration. In the real world we would have to have a definition of what a Photo object is in the first place, called a *class*, before we could create an *instance* of it. If we were to run the preceding code as is, we would get an error. We'll discuss classes more at the end of this chapter, in the section called "PHP Classes and Objects."

PHP Operators

The next basic feature of the PHP language that we will examine is the *operator*. Operators are used to take existing values, also called *expressions*, and transform them into new values. They can be used for comparing values, performing arithmetic, and manipulating data. In other words, they are used to operate on data.

We've already come across a couple of operators in this chapter, the concatenation operator (.) and the assignment operator (=). There are many others, some of them more esoteric than others. For instance, there is the concatenating assignment operator, which is a hybrid of the concatenation and the assignment operators. It is used to append a new value to the value already assigned to a variable, as the following code illustrates:

```php
<?php
$sandwich = "peanut butter";
$sandwich .= " and jelly";
echo $sandwich;
?>
```

```
peanut butter and jelly
```

First we assigned a value to the $sandwich variable, using the assignment operator, then we appended a second value to $sandwich using the concatenating assignment operator.

We are not going to describe all of the operators here, but we are going to describe some frequently used ones that you will need to know for the examples in this book.

First, let's take a look at the arithmetic operators.

```php
<?php
$a = 5;
$b = 11;

$sum = $a + $b;   // addition operator +
$difference = $a - $b;   // subtraction operator -
$product = $a * $b; // multiplication operator *
$quotient = $a / $b; // quotient operator /
$remainder = $a % $b;   // modulus operator %

echo "$a + $b = $sum <br/>";
echo "$a - $b = $difference <br/>";
echo "$a x $b = $product <br/>";
echo "$a / $b = $quotient <br/>";
echo "$a mod $b = $remainder <br/>";
?>
```

Following are the results:

```
5 + 11 = 16
5 - 11 = -6
5 x 11 = 55
5 / 11 = 0.45454545454545
5 mod 11 = 5
```

In the previous example, we used various operators to add, subtract, multiply, and divide, as well as to find the remainder of one number divided by another. We can also use operators to compare values. Comparison operators return either TRUE or FALSE, based on the results of the comparison of two values.

```php
<?php
$a = 7; // Assignment operator. Sets the value of $a to 7.
$b = 12;

/*
Equal operator. True if $a is equal to $b, regardless of the data type of values.
If $a = '3' and $b = 3, this will return TRUE.
*/
$a == $b;
```

```
/*
Identical operator. True if $a is equal to $b and if they are the same data type.
If $a = '3' and $b = 3, this will return FALSE.
*/
$a === $b;

$a != $b; // Not equal operator. True if $a is not equal to $b.
$a <> $b; // Also a not equal operator. True if $a not equal to $b.

/*
Not identical operator.
True if $a is not equal to $b or if they are not of the same type.
*/
$a !== $b;

$a < $b; // Less-than operator. True if $a < $b.
$a > $b; // Greater-than operator. True if $a > $b.
$a <= $b; // Less-than-or-equal-to operator.
          // True if $a is less than or equal to $b.
$a >= $b; // Greater-than-or-equal-to operator.
          // True if $a is greater than or equal to $b.
?>
```

Another type of operator that you'll want to be familiar with is the logical operator. Logical operators examine the Boolean value of the expression.

```
<?php
$a = TRUE;
$b = FALSE;

$a && $b;
$a || $b;
$a xor $b; // XOR
!$a; // Not
?>
```

The final operators we will look at are the increment and decrement operators. These operators are used to add 1 to the current value of a variable or subtract 1 from the current value, respectively.

```
<?php
$a = 7;
echo $a . "<br/>";

$a++;
echo $a . "<br/>";

$a--;
echo $a ."<br/>";
?>
```

Following is what the code produces:

```
7
8
7
```

PHP Control Structures

Computer programs are orderly creatures. They like to do things systematically, one step at a time, completing one task, then going on to the next. This movement from one instruction to the next is called the *program flow*.

Now that we know more about variables, expressions, and operators, we can start putting these pieces together into more complex structures that control the flow of a program. These structures are called *control structures*. By building control structures, a programmer can make the flow of a program loop over the same piece of code to repeat a tedious task, fork between different options to make decisions, or stop completely to end the code.

Control structures are blocks of code that begin with if, do, switch, while, or for. They are usually followed by a *conditional expression*, which is made up of values and operators. Then they have curly braces to hold together the code in the structure.

The best way to understand what they are is to see an example. So let's look at a very important control structure, the if structure.

if/elseif/else

The if structure allows for conditional execution of code. In other words, it allows code to run *if* a certain criterion is met. Let's look at an example:

```php
<?php

$count = 5;

if ($count == 5) {
  echo "There are $count photos in this set.";
}

if ($count == 4) {
  echo "This statement will be ignored.";
}

?>
```

Following is the result:

```
There are 5 photos in this set.
```

In the preceding example, we assign the value 5 to the variable $count. Next, using an if state-ment, we check to see whether $count is equal to 5. Since it is, the code inside of the curly braces executes and displays the resulting text. In the second if statement, we check to see whether $count is equal to 4, which it is not, so the statement in this if block is ignored. Notice that the if statement itself does not use a semicolon to separate it from the other code. Only the statements inside of the braces use semicolons.

　　　Instead of using two separate if statements, we could have used the elseif statement to combine this into one if statement:

```php
<?php

$count = 4;

if ($count == 5) {
   echo "There are $count photos in this set.";
} elseif ($count == 4) {
   echo "This statement will not be ignored.";
}

?>
```

Following is the result:

```
This statement will not be ignored.
```

In the preceding example, we changed $count to 4. When the code executes, it looks at the first part of the if statement. Since $count is not equal to 5, the first echo statement is ignored. Next, the program goes to the elseif statement. Since this conditional expression ($count = 4) is TRUE, the code here executes, and the output from the second echo statement is returned.

　　　You can also have the option of using the else clause, which applies when the conditions in the previous if or elseif statements are not fulfilled. For instance, if we use the previous example and tack on an else statement, we get the following:

```php
<?php
$count = 7;

if ($count == 5) {
   echo "There are $count photos in this set.";
} elseif ($count == 4) {
   echo "This statement will be ignored.";
} else {
   echo "The count is not equal to 4 or 5.";
}
?>
```

Following is the result:

```
The count is not equal to 4 or 5.
```

In the preceding example, we changed the $count to 7. Since it is not 5 or 4, the if and elseif clauses of this statement are ignored, and the code execution flows to the default else clause and echoes those results.

switch/case

The if structure works well when there are only a few conditions, or cases, to be evaluated. When there are more than a few options, we can use the switch/case structure instead. A switch/case statement works by first evaluating an expression, then jumping to a particular block of code based on the results.

```php
<?php
$color="blue";

switch ($color) {
  case "orange":
    echo "This is orange.";
    break;
  case "blue":
    echo "This is blue.";
    break;
  case "green":
    echo "This is green.";
    break;
  case "red":
    echo "This is red.";
    break;
}
?>
```

Following is the result:

```
This is blue.
```

When the preceding block of code is run, the engine evaluates the value of $color. It then goes down the list of cases, looking for a match. If it finds one, it executes the code until it reaches the break statement, which ends the execution of the switch block. In this case, since we have assigned "blue" to the $color variable, the engine looks at the first case (case "orange") and ignores it. Then it looks at the next case (case "blue") and finds a match. It then executes the echo statement that follows, then breaks. The rest of the cases are ignored, since a match has already been found and the break statement has been executed.

What if we want to have a catch-all case that gets executed if none of the others do? This can be done using the default keyword:

```php
<?php
$color="chartreuse";

switch ($color) {
  case "orange":
    echo "This is orange.";
    break;
  case "blue":
    echo "This is blue.";
    break;
  case "green":
    echo "This is green.";
    break;
  case "red":
    echo "This is red.";
    break;
  default:
    echo "This color isn't recognized.";
    break;
}
?>
```

Following is the result:

```
This color isn't recognized.
```

In the preceding example, we used a color (chartreuse) that wasn't specified by any of the cases, so the engine executes the default case and then exits.

while and do/while

Another type of control structure is the loop. Loops are used to repeat a set of instructions several times, until a specified condition is met. The while statement is used to create one kind of loop. As its name implies, it executes a piece of code while a condition is met. It looks like the following:

```php
<?php
$count = 1;
while ( $count < 4 ) {
  echo "The value of \$count is now $count. <br/>";
  $count++;
}
?>
```

Following are the results:

```
The value of $count is now 1.
The value of $count is now 2.
The value of $count is now 3.
```

In the preceding example, we set the value of $count to 1. Next, the program checks the value of $count to see if it is less than 4. Since $count is less than 4, it runs the code in the statement block. First it echoes a few words and the current value of $count, then in the next statement it increments the value of $count using the increment operator (++). The value of $count is now 2, and the while statement starts again. The code runs until the $count variable has a value of 4. Notice that we've used the escape character (\) to escape the dollar sign in the string. So, instead of printing the variable's value, we print its name.

An alternate form of the while loop is the do/while loop. Instead of evaluating the value of $count before the loop has begun, the do/while loop checks the value at the end.

```php
<?php
$count = 6;
do {
    echo "The value of \$count is now $count. <br/>";
    $count++;
} while ($count < 4);
?>
```

Following is the result:

```
The value of $count is now 6.
```

Using a do/while structure ensures that the loop runs at least once, no matter what the value of $count is. So if $count were 6 to begin with, the code would run one time before the engine discovered that $count was in fact greater than 5.

Keep in mind when constructing a loop that you must create a condition for the loop to end, or it will run indefinitely in an endless loop.

for

Another kind of loop that you'll come across frequently is the for loop. The for loop allows a programmer to set more complex criteria for the way the loop is run. The syntax of the for loop is similar to that of the while loop, but it starts off with three expressions rather than just one. The syntax is as follows:

```php
for (expr1; expr2; expr3){
    statements;
}
```

The first expression (expr1) is executed only the first time the loop is evaluated. The second expression (expr2) is evaluated at the beginning of each loop and determines whether or not the loop should run again. Finally, the last expression is executed at the end of each iteration of the loop. In practice, the for loop often looks something like the following:

```php
<?php
for ($counter = 1; $counter < 4; $counter++) {
   echo "The counter is set to $counter.<br/>";
}
?>
```

Following is the result:

```
The counter is set to 1.
The counter is set to 2.
The counter is set to 3.
```

The preceding code is an example of a loop that will run three times. The first time through the loop, $counter is set to 1. Next, $counter is checked to see whether it is less than 4. Since it is, the loop is executed. At the end of the loop, $counter is incremented. Then the process starts again, except that $counter is not initially set to 1 again.

foreach

A final type of loop is the foreach loop. This is the kind of loop you'll want to use when you need to iterate through the members of an array. For instance, let's say we have an array called $photographers, which we want to list the contents of. We can use the foreach array to do this as follows:

```php
<?php
$photographers = array("Ansel Adams", "Diane Arbus", "Lee Freidlander", ➥
    "Robert Doisneau", "Alvin Langdon Coburn", "William Eggleston");
foreach ($photographers as $p) {
   echo $p."<br/>";
}
?>
```

Following is the result:

```
Ansel Adams
Diane Arbus
Lee Freidlander
Robert Doisneau
Alvin Langdon Coburn
William Eggleston
```

What's going on here? First we define the $photographers array. Then using the foreach statement, we assign the first value in the $photographers array to variable $p. The loop then proceeds, and the echo statement is processed. On the next iteration of the loop, the second value from the $photographers array is put into the $p variable. This continues until all of the values in the array have been used. So when we use the foreach statement, we are in effect saying, "for each value in this array, perform the following instructions."

PHP Includes and Requires

When working on a big coding project, it is helpful to break up the code into separate files in order to keep things organized. Later, when you need to use some of the code stored in one of the files, you just refer to that file to get the code you need. To do this, you use either the include or require statement. In practice, it looks like this:

```
<?php
include "filename.php";
?>
```

So when should one use include instead of require? Include and require do exactly the same thing, with one exception. If the file specified in the include statement cannot be found, the PHP engine will return a warning and keep running, but a require statement will return a fatal error and force the PHP engine to stop executing.

Another variation of the include and require statements are the include_once and require_once statements. These statements allow code to be included only once per execution. This is important when you are using variables or objects that you don't want to have redefined. This is especially useful when using objects in your code.

PHP Functions

Functions are programming structures that allow a programmer to avoid rewriting the same code over and over again. Using a function, a programmer can group code under a specific name, then use that code just by writing the function name in the program. This is known as "calling" a function.

Functions are usually defined at the beginning of a program.

```
<?php
function doSomething() {
  echo "This is the first step in the function.<br/>";
  echo "This is the next step.<br/>";
}

echo "This is the first line of the program.<br/>";

doSomething();

echo "Let's run the function again.<br/>";

doSomething();

echo "This is the end of the program.<br/>";
?>
```

Following is the result:

```
This is the first line of the program.
This is the first step in the function.
This is the next step.
Let's run the function again.
This is the first step in the function.
This is the next step.
This is the end of the program.
```

First the engine executes the first line of the program. When it comes across the doSomething() function call, code execution jumps to the first line of the doSomething() function. When the function completes, code execution returns to the spot where it left off, and the main program continues.

PHP Classes and Objects

The earliest computer programs were simply a list of instructions which would tell a computer what to do, one step at a time. While these basic programs were satisfactory for machines that performed only a few simple tasks, like calculating artillery trajectories, they were somewhat limiting as computers became more complex and capable.

Eventually, the programming paradigm evolved to allow for *procedural programming*. In the procedural programming paradigm, in addition to a simple list of instructions, the programs could also contain procedures, or functions. As we have seen, functions allow the programmer to write a piece of code that can be used over and over, and to separate it from the main set of instructions. To use the function, you simply call it from the main program, and it springs into action and performs a task. After the task is performed, the main program continues about its business. This allowed programmers to write code that was modular and reusable. Say, for instance, you wanted your program to add two numbers together. If someone had already written the add() function, there would be no need for you to write it again. If there wasn't an add() function yet, you could write it yourself; then it would be available for other programmers to use.

While procedural programming allowed for great strides in the speed in which code could be written, recent advancements in technology have demanded more sophisticated tasks to be performed by code. It became necessary to have a programming paradigm that made it easy not only to perform actions but also to create complex models and simulations. This recent evolution in the way people program computers is known as object-oriented programming, or OOP for short.

In the OOP paradigm, most of the code in a program is neatly packaged into individual units called classes. From classes, a programmer can create individual instances called objects. Objects are somewhat self-contained; they can store information about themselves, and they also contain functions that they can perform.

Earlier in this chapter, we touched very briefly upon on OOP when we were describing the object data type. We know that PHP can store objects in a variable the way it can store a number or a piece of text. We know that objects can have properties and functions, but we were a little vague on where objects come from, and how they get properties and functions.

In our earlier example, we assigned a Photo object to the variable $p using the new keyword and then gave the Photo object some values. To refresh your memory:

```php
<?php
// Dummy class definition.
class Photo {
  function savePhoto() {
    // code to save the photo goes here
  }
}

$p = new Photo();

$p->id = '5859628';
$p->title = 'This is a test photo.';
$p->URL = 'http://photos3.flickr.com/5859628_64c58f62a3.jpg';
$p->savePhoto();

echo $p->id."<br/>";
echo $p->title."<br/>";
?>

<a href="<?php echo $p->URL; ?>"><?php echo $p->URL; ?></a><br/>
```

What we didn't explain was how it was decided that Photo objects should have an id, a title, and a URL. And where did that savePhoto() function come from anyway? Let's examine that now. Also note how this time we've built a link from the photo's URL by embedding PHP into the HTML.

All objects are described by classes. A *class* is a prototype of an object, a sort of object template that all of the other objects are created from. If you've ever had a Philosophy 101 course in college, you might remember Plato's forms, which were the perfect versions of the things we encounter in our daily lives. Classes are similar; they provide a definition from which objects with individual variations are created. Once an object is created, it's on its own and can be altered and adjusted within the parameters that describe it.

So let's take a look at an extremely simplified version of the Photo class.

```php
<?php
class Photo {

  public $id = 0;
  public $title = '';
  public $URL = '';

  function showValues() {
    echo $this->id;
    echo $this->title;
    echo $this->URL;
  }
```

```
  function savePhoto() {
    // code to save the photo goes here
  }
}
?>
```

In the preceding code you can see the basic layout of a PHP class. It begins with the variables or properties that all the objects created from this class will have. So all Photo objects created from this class will have an id, a title, and a URL. The value set represents the default values that all objects created from the class will have when they are first created. In this case, all Photo objects have a default id value of 0 and have a blank title and URL.

Our example class also has two functions defined: the showValues() function and the savePhoto() function. For the sake of simplicity, we've left out the code that would actually save the photo, but in the showValues() function, we put in some code to return the values of an individual object's variables. Notice that when we are describing a variable inside the class, we can use the $this keyword to describe a variable of that particular object. So say we create three different objects using this class and call the showValues() function on each object. The $this keyword instructs PHP to return the id, title, and URL for each particular object.

While there is much more that can be said about PHP objects and classes, the preceding example should be sufficient to help you identify a PHP class when you come across one in the examples in following chapters. The important thing to understand is that classes act as a template that defines all objects created from the class. When you create an object, it will have default values that you can change and adjust, and functions that you can put to use. Throughout this book we will be creating objects from existing classes and using the functions defined in those classes, but we will not be changing the classes themselves.

Summary

In this chapter, we've taken a whirlwind, whistle-stop tour of the PHP language. We've identified the most basic features of the language and pointed out how to recognize them when you come across them in the code examples of chapters that follow.

As we mentioned in the beginning of this chapter, we don't expect you to be a programming expert to be able to make use good of this book. It's our hope that this book can be a helpful companion to someone interested in learning the PHP language and using the advanced features of the Flickr website. To fully understand the PHP language, we highly recommend that you consult the thorough online documentation provided by the official PHP site (http://www.php.net).

In the next chapter, we'll take what we've covered here and put it to use by taking photos from your Flickr account and displaying them on your website.

CHAPTER 5

Worth a Thousand Words: Working with Flickr Photos

Once you have a handle on the basics of PHP and have a good idea of what Flickr is all about, you're ready to start programming with the Flickr API. In this chapter we'll do just that by using the Phlickr PHP library to connect to the Flickr website and access a single photo in your account.

Quick Start: A Photo on Your Web Page

For a quick start, we'll make a web page that displays one of your Flickr photos. This example assumes that you have a local web server running PHP and that you've installed the Phlickr libraries. You also need the authentication token file that tells Flickr who you are and allows you to access your account. Instructions for setting up your computer and creating an authentication token can be found in Chapter 3.

Try It Out: Placing a Flickr Photo in a Web Page

If you're already set up, simply place the file below on your web server and view it in a browser:

```php
<?php
//show_photo.php

define('API_CONFIG_FILE', './authtoken.dat');

include_once 'Phlickr/Api.php';
include_once 'Phlickr/Photo.php';

$photoid = '4285703';

$api = Phlickr_Api::createFrom(API_CONFIG_FILE);
if (! $api->isAuthValid()) {
  die('invalid flickr logon');
}
```

```
$p = new Phlickr_Photo($api, $photoid);
?>

<html>
  <head>
    <title>Display a Photo</title>
  </head>

  <body>
    <br/>
    <h1 align="center"><?php echo $p->getTitle(); ?></h1>
    <p align="center"><img src="<?php echo $p->buildImgUrl('-'); ?>" /></p>
  </body>
</html>
```

When you open this page you should get something that looks like Figure 5-1.

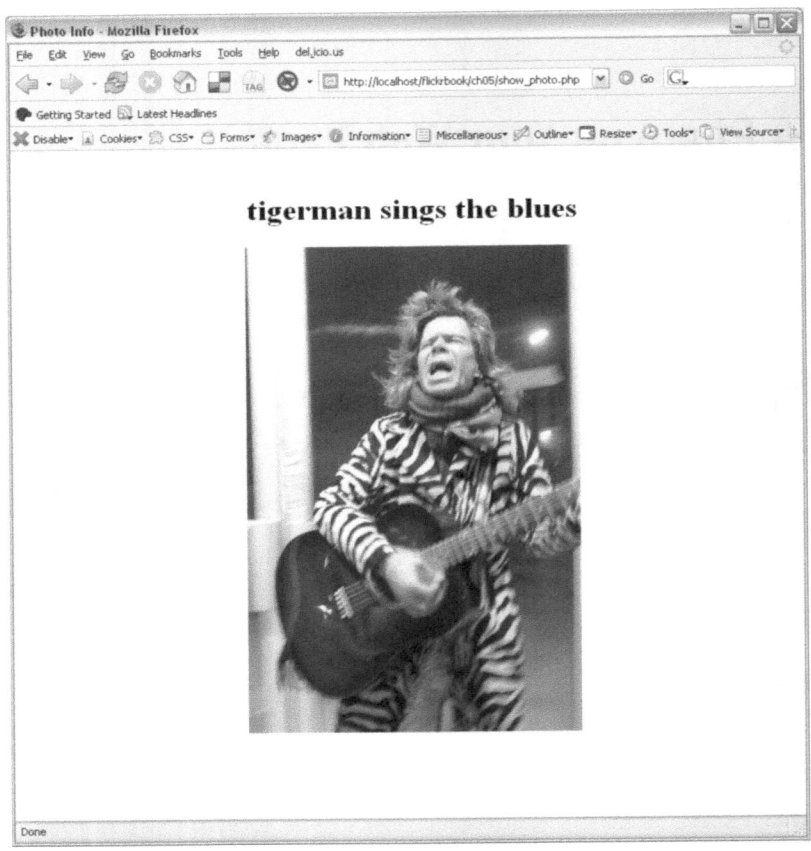

Figure 5-1. *A simple web page displaying a Flickr photo*

How It Works

The first line of code defines the constant `API_CONFIG_FILE` and sets the value of the constant to the location where we stored the configuration file. This file contains the authentication information that you will need in order to connect to Flickr.

```
define('API_CONFIG_FILE', './authtoken.dat');
```

Next we include the Phlickr classes that we will need to access a photo, namely the `Phlickr_Api` class and the `Phlickr_Photo` class.

```
include_once 'Phlickr/Api.php';
include_once 'Phlickr/Photo.php';
```

Then we define the variable `$photoid` and set it to the ID of the photo we want to look up. In this case it's the photo with the ID 4285703. You can determine the photo ID for one of your own photos by visiting the photo's page on Flickr. You will see a URL that looks something like: http://www.flickr.com/photos/goodlux/118555758/. The number at the end of the URL is the ID number of that particular photo.

```
$photoid = '4285703';
```

Now that we've supplied the values for the variables and included the classes, we create a connection to the API.

```
$api = Phlickr_Api::createFrom(API_CONFIG_FILE);

if (! $api->isAuthValid()) {
  die('invalid flickr logon');
}
```

If for some reason PHP cannot connect to Flickr, the code will exit with the "invalid flickr logon" message. Once we've created the API connection, we can create a new photo object and set it to the ID we've provided.

```
$p = new Phlickr_Photo($api, $photoid);
```

From here, we use three methods to get information about the photo and echo the results to the browser enclosed in HTML tags so they display properly. Note the `buildImgUrl()` that builds a URL that is suitable for an `<img>` tag.

```
<html>
  <head>
    <title>Display a Photo</title>
  </head>

  <body>
    <br/>
    <h1 align="center"><?php echo $p->getTitle(); ?></h1>
    <p align="center"><img src="<?php echo $p->buildImgUrl('-'); ?>" /></p>
  </body>
</html>
```

A Closer Look at the Phlickr_Photo Class

There are a few steps involved in working with a photo object. The first thing that you will need to do is create a connection to the Flickr website, called an API connection. This connection establishes your identity with Flickr and opens a communication channel where you can describe the objects you want to use and tell Flickr what to do with them.

When you've established a connection, the next step is to create a new photo object. Once you have a new, blank photo object, you tell Flickr exactly which photo you want this object to represent by providing its photo ID number. You then can access all of the properties of the particular photo: its title, its URL, the time it was created and uploaded, and more.

Try It Out: Accessing the Properties of a Photo

Let's see what this looks like in code.

```php
<?php
//photo_info.php

define('API_CONFIG_FILE', './authtoken.dat');

include_once 'Phlickr/Api.php';
include_once 'Phlickr/Photo.php';

$photoid = '19481086';

$api = Phlickr_Api::createFrom(API_CONFIG_FILE);
if (! $api->isAuthValid()) {
  die('invalid flickr logon');
}

$p = new Phlickr_Photo($api, $photoid);
?>

<html>
  <head>
    <title>Photo Info</title>
  </head>

  <body>
    <p>
```

```php
<img src="<?php echo $p->buildImgUrl('m'); ?> " /><br/>
Some quick facts about this photo:<br/>
photo id: <?php echo $p->getId(); ?><br/>
photo title: <?php echo $p->getTitle(); ?><br/>
photo description: <?php echo $p->getDescription(); ?><br/>
this photo was uploaded by user id: <?php echo $p->getUserId(); ?><br/>
you can find the flickr photo page for this image at:
   <?php echo $p->buildUrl(); ?><br/>
you can find just the image file at: <?php echo $p->buildImgUrl(); ?><br/>
this photo was taken on: <?php echo $p->getTakenDate(); ?><br/>
the timestamp when taken was: <?php echo $p->getTakenTimestamp(); ?><br/>
the granularity of the taken timestamp is:
   <?php echo $p->getTakenGranularity(); ?><br/>
this photo was posted on: <?php echo $p->getPostedDate(); ?><br/>
the timestamp when posted was: <?php echo $p->getPostedTimestamp(); ?><br/>
this photo secret is: <?php echo $p->getSecret(); ?><br/>
this photo is hosted on flickr server number:
   <?php echo $p->getServer(); ?><br/>
can this photo be seen by family?: <?php echo $p->isForFamily(); ?><br/>
can this photo be seen by friends?: <?php echo $p->isForFriends(); ?><br/>
can this photo be seen by everyone?: <?php echo $p->isForPublic(); ?><br/>
photo sizes: <?php echo $p->getSizes(); ?><br/>
raw tags: <?php echo $p->getRawTags(); ?><br/>
regular tags: <?php echo $p->getTags(); ?><br/>
        </p>
      </body>
</html>
```

When viewing this file in a web browser, you will get something that looks like Figure 5-2:

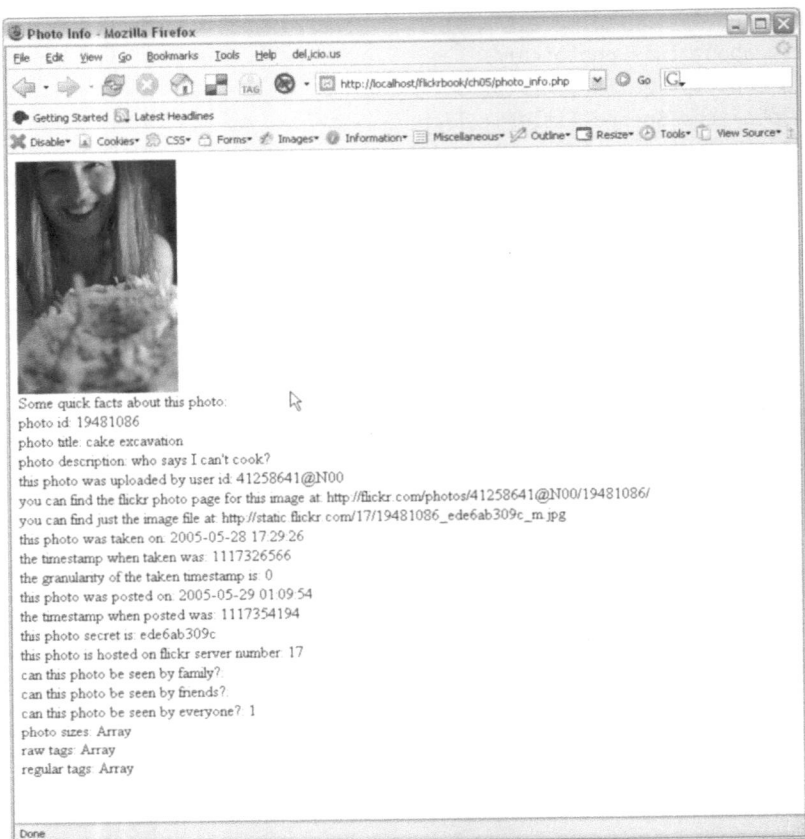

Figure 5-2. *Extracting a photograph's information*

How It Works

This example is very similar to our first example, but in this case we've gone through many of the methods of the Phlickr_Photo object and sent the results to the browser. We do this by escaping out of the HTML code back to PHP to call the method.

```
photo id: <?php echo $p->getId(); ?><br/>
```

Some Notes on the Results from the Phlickr_Photo Class

While some of the results from the previous example are fairly straightforward, others benefit from a little explanation. For instance, the getId() method obviously just spits out the ID of the photo, but why are there two different URLs for the same photo? Also, "Array" is not a very useful result. We'll explain the trickier ones here.

Why You Need Two (or More) URLs for the Same Photo

First, you might have noticed that there are two different methods for getting the URL of a particular image. There are the `buildUrl()` and `buildImgUrl()` methods. The first method, `buildUrl()`, gets the URL that you are most familiar with, the one that you normally see when you look at a photo on Flickr. The second method, `buildImgUrl()`, is much more useful. It gets the URL of just the image file. You can use this URL to display the photo in your own web page with the formatting you like. You can also choose which image size you want from the selection that Flickr has available by supplying an optional parameter. The options are shown in Table 5-1:

Table 5-1. *Image Size Parameters*

Size	Dimensions	Parameter
Square	75×75 pixels	s
Thumbnail	Longest side 100 pixels	t
Small	Longest side 240 pixels	m
Medium	Longest side 500 pixels	default: leave blank or -
Large	Longest side 1,024 pixels	b
Original	Same as original file uploaded	o

So if you want the thumbnail for the image in question, use the `buildImgUrl()` method with the t parameter, or `buildImgUrl('t')`. Beware that the parameters don't seem to match up with the names: for instance, the small size uses the m parameter, and large size is called using b. Also keep in mind that if your original file is not at least 1,024 pixels on the longest side, you won't be able to use the large size. We'll take a look at this later in the chapter when we display the images in a web page.

Timestamps and Timestamp Granularity

The date and time the photo was taken and the date and time the photo was uploaded can be provided as a Unix timestamp as well as the much more readable MySQL DATETIME format. The Unix timestamp is actually the number of seconds that have passed since January 1, 1970 GMT. If you've just started programming, this might not seem to be very useful information, but it comes in handy when working with many PHP functions.

You will notice also that the time the photo was taken has a timestamp *granularity*, which is the level of detail recorded. This is necessary information, because you may not know for sure exactly when you took a picture, especially if you are uploading scanned images that you took with your old film camera. You might know only that you took a photo in a certain year or month, so the exact time you took these photos can't be known.

Presently, only the three values shown in Table 5-2 are used for granularity.

Table 5-2. *Photo Timestamp Granularity*

Granularity	Precision
0	Y-m-d H:i:s
4	Y-m
6	Y

So a photo that was taken some time in June 1980 would have a taken date of 1980-06-01 00:00:00 and a granularity of 4. In the future, Flickr may add additional values to these three, in the range from 0–10.

Photos and Their Secrets

To build the URL that links to the static image file, you need to have three pieces of information: the number of the server that the image resides on, the image's ID, and the photo secret. When put together, you get a URL that looks like this: `http://static.flickr.com/17/19481086_ede6ab309c.jpg`.

In this case, 17 is the server number, 19481086 is the photo ID, and ede6ab309c is the photo secret.

The photo secret is available only to people that have permission to view the photo. So if you have blocked everyone from viewing an image that you have stored on Flickr, you can still make this image available to your website or blog, even if it isn't visible in your photostream. This helps you keep your photostream uncluttered with images that aren't meant for other Flickr users in particular.

Who Can View This Photo?

The `isForFamily()`, `isForFriends()`, and `isForPublic()` functions all return a Boolean value; they are either TRUE or FALSE. So a "1" in the results means TRUE, and the photo is visible. These values are assigned based on the privacy selections that the owner of the photo has specified.

Array Results

Finally, you will notice that the `getSizes()`, `getRawTags()`, and `getTags()` functions all return arrays for their results. The easiest way to just see the values stored in the arrays is to use the `print_r()` function. This simply dumps the contents of the array to the screen so you can see what is stored within. Let's try this using the same photo from the previous example. This time we'll use the command line, because it's easier to see the array's structure in command-line output:

```php
<?php
//get_sizes.php

define('API_CONFIG_FILE', './authtoken.dat');

include_once 'Phlickr/Api.php';
include_once 'Phlickr/Photo.php';

$photoid = '19481086';

$api = Phlickr_Api::createFrom(API_CONFIG_FILE);
if (! $api->isAuthValid()) {
  die('invalid flickr logon');
}
```

```php
$p = new Phlickr_Photo($api, $photoid);

$sizes = $p->getSizes();
$rawtags = $p->getRawTags();
$tags = $p->getTags();

echo "The results of the getSizes() method are...\r\n";
print_r ( $p->getSizes());

echo "The results of the getRawTags() method are...\r\n";
print_r ($p->getRawTags());

echo "The results of the getTags() method are...\r\n";
print_r ($p->getTags());
?>
```

When run from the command line, you will get the following results:

```
$ php get_sizes.php
```

```
The results of the getSizes() method are...
Array
(
    [s] => Array
        (
            [0] => 75
            [1] => 75
            [type] => jpg
        )

    [t] => Array
        (
            [0] => 67
            [1] => 100
            [type] => jpg
        )

    [m] => Array
        (
            [0] => 160
            [1] => 240
            [type] => jpg
        )
```

```
    [-] => Array
        (
            [0] => 333
            [1] => 500
            [type] => jpg
        )

    [o] => Array
        (
            [0] => 533
            [1] => 800
            [type] => jpg
        )

)
The results of the getRawTags() method are...
Array
(
    [0] => birthday
    [1] => beth
)
The results of the getTags() method are...
Array
(
    [0] => birthday
    [1] => beth
)
```

You can see from the results that the getSizes() function returns an array that has arrays for its values—arrays within an array. Each member of the resulting array contains an array with three values: the horizontal dimension, the vertical dimension, and the type of image, respectively. Notice in this case that there are s, t, m, -, and o sizes, but there is no b or large size. This is because the original size file was only 800 pixels on its longest side, which is smaller than the minimum requirement of 1,024 pixels for a large image size, so a large image size is not available for this image.

The getRawTags() and getTags() methods seem to return the same values, and in fact they do return the same values in this case. The difference between these two methods is that the getRawTags() method will return tags with any non-alphanumeric characters intact. Most of the time while programming this is undesirable; usually you will want only the tag without any extra spaces or special characters, so the getTags() method is generally more useful.

Another Way of Working with HTML

Our first example uses PHP running on the web server to display an image from Flickr in a webpage. If your web host supports PHP 5, you will easily be able to run the example. However, at the time of this writing PHP 5 is still in its early phases of mainstream adoption, and you might not have access to PHP 5 and Phlickr on your server. If this is your situation, don't fret. You can still use PHP 5 and Phlickr to make your web pages. You just need to run PHP 5 locally on your home computer and have your scripts produce static HTML pages. You can then upload your newly created web pages to the server with an FTP program.

This technique of creating pages locally and uploading to a web server has two additional advantages. First, since the pages aren't dynamic, they are faster because they don't have to connect through the Flickr API each time the page is viewed. This makes a noticeable difference when working with large sets of photos. Second, the Flickr terms of service require that you create a link back to the individual photo page when using an image hosted on Flickr's servers. Perhaps you've created a site where you don't want a user to click on an image and jump back to the Flickr page, but you like using Flickr to easily manage your photo sets. By creating a static page locally based on the set, then automatically uploading the page and the associated photos to your web host, you can create a site that doesn't link back to Flickr and can still remain within the terms of your user agreement.

Try It Out: Making a Static HTML Page Using the Phlickr Libraries

It's simple. Let's convert our initial example to a static HTML page.

```php
<?php
//make_html.php

define('API_CONFIG_FILE', './authtoken.dat');

include_once 'Phlickr/Api.php';
include_once 'Phlickr/Photo.php';

$savepath = 'c:/html/';

$htmlfilename = 'photopage.html';

$photoid = '71738376';

$api = Phlickr_Api::createFrom(API_CONFIG_FILE);
if (! $api->isAuthValid()) {
  die('invalid flickr logon');
}

$p = new Phlickr_Photo($api, $photoid);

$html = "<html>\r\n";
$html = $html."<br/>\n";
$html = $html."<h1>".$p->getTitle()."</h1>\r\n";
$html = $html."<img src=".$p->buildImgUrl()." />\r\n";
$html = $html."<h3>".$p->getDescription()."</h3>\r\n";
$html = $html."</html>\r\n";

$f = $savepath.$htmlfilename;
file_put_contents($f, $html);
?>
```

After you run the script, you should see a file called photopage.html in the path specified in the $savepath variable. In this case, you'll find the file in c:\html. If you view the file in a text editor, you will see the following HTML (there was no description of this photo, so nothing in the <h3> tags):

```
<html>
<br/>
<h1>Monkey Man of Ubud, Bali</h1>
<img src=http://static.flickr.com/34/71738376_f98429b9b5_m.jpg />
<h3></h3>
</html>
```

You can now upload this file to your web server to display the image.

How It Works

This example is exactly the same as our first example, except instead of writing the output to the browser directly, we write it to a file locally. To do this we use the PHP file handling function file_put_contents(). This file can then be uploaded to the web server for normal viewing.

Downloading a Photo

A common task is to download the actual image file. We could, for example, download all of the images associated with our static web page in the preceding example. This can also be easily accomplished using PHP's file_get_contents() function.

Try It Out: Downloading an Image File

Let's go ahead and download an image. Since downloading a file involves the file system, we'll use the command line again.

```php
<?php
//save_image.php

define('API_CONFIG_FILE', './authtoken.dat');

include_once 'Phlickr/Api.php';
include_once 'Phlickr/Photo.php';

// get the photo id from the command line
$cmdarg = $_SERVER['argv'];
$photoid = $cmdarg[1];

$savedirectory = 'C:/images/';

$api = Phlickr_Api::createFrom(API_CONFIG_FILE);
if (! $api->isAuthValid()) {
  die('invalid flickr logon');
}
```

```php
$p = new Phlickr_Photo($api, $photoid);

$url = $p->buildImgUrl('o');

$imagefile = file_get_contents($url);

$localfile = $savedirectory.'myimage.jpg';
file_put_contents($localfile, $imagefile);

echo "file saved...";
?>
```

Run the script as follows, by supplying a photo ID at the command line:

```
$ php save_image.php 4285701
```

When you run this code, if all goes well, you will get a simple message telling you "file saved...."
If you look in the save directory you've specified with the $savedirectory variable, you will see a
file called myimage.jpg. This is the original-sized file that you've downloaded from Flickr.

How It Works

In this example, we take the list of command-line arguments ($_SERVER['argv']) and select
the second one. (The first one, $cmdarg[0], is the name of the PHP script we are running.)

```php
$cmdarg = $_SERVER['argv'];
$photoid = $cmdarg[1];
```

We then create a Phlickr_Photo object using the ID supplied. We use the PHP
file_get_contents() function to grab an image file. In this case, the URL that we pass to
the function comes from the Phlickr buildImgUrl() function. The image file is temporarily
stored in the variable $imagefile. We write this image file to the local file system using
PHP's file_put_contents() function.

Using the Phlickr_AuthedPhoto Class

In addition to the Phlickr_Photo class, the Phlickr library also has a class called the
Phlickr_AuthedPhoto class, which is an extension of the Phlickr_Photo class. Both of these classes
serve a different purpose. When you are writing code that will look at other people's photos as well
as your own, you will want to use the Phlickr_Photo class. The Phlickr_AuthedPhoto class is for use
when you are working exclusively with your own photos. The Phlickr_AuthedPhoto class requires
you to be logged in and to be the owner of the photo, and it allows you to alter the photo metadata
directly.

In addition to the methods we demonstrated earlier in the chapter, you gain the following
methods when using the Phlickr_AuthedPhoto class:

- setMeta()
- setPosted()
- setTags()
- setTaken()

Try It Out: Getting More Information About a Photo

Let's try these out with a simple example:

```php
<?php
//more_info.php

define('API_CONFIG_FILE', './authtoken.dat');

include_once 'Phlickr/Api.php';
include_once 'Phlickr/AuthedPhoto.php';

$photoid = '88660990'; //make sure you pick a photo that you own

$api = Phlickr_Api::createFrom(API_CONFIG_FILE);

if (! $api->isAuthValid()) {
  die('invalid flickr logon');
}

$p = new Phlickr_AuthedPhoto($api, $photoid);

$original_title = $p->getTitle();
$original_description = $p->getDescription();
$original_posted_time = $p->getPostedDate();
$original_taken_time = $p->getTakenDate();
$original_tags = $p->getTags();

$p->setMeta('This is the new Title', 'This is the new Description');
$p->setPosted(mktime (8,15,23,3,4,03));
$p->setTaken(mktime (2,34,54,6,6,99));
$p->setTags(array('specialphoto','cameraphone', 'testphotos'));

$new_title = $p->getTitle();
$new_description = $p->getDescription();
$new_posted_time = $p->getPostedDate();
$new_taken_time = $p->getTakenDate();
$new_tags = $p->getTags();
?>

<html>
  <head>
    <title>Setting and Getting Photo Info</title>
  </head>
```

```
<body>
  <p>
    The original title was: <?php echo $original_title; ?><br/>
    The new title is: <?php echo $new_title; ?><br/>
    The original description was: <?php echo $original_description; ?><br/>
    The new decription is: <?php echo $new_description; ?><br/>
    The original time taken was: <?php echo $original_taken_time; ?><br/>
    The new time taken is: <?php echo $new_taken_time; ?><br/>
    The original time posted was: <?php echo $original_posted_time; ?><br/>
    The new time posted is: <?php echo $new_posted_time; ?><br/>
    The original tags were:<br/>
    <pre>
      <?php echo print_r ($original_tags); ?>
    </pre><br/>
    The new tags are:<br/>
    <pre>
      <?php echo print_r ($new_tags); ?>
    </pre>
  </p>
</body>
</html>
```

If you save the preceding code to a file on your web server and view it in a browser, you should get the following results (see Figure 5-3).

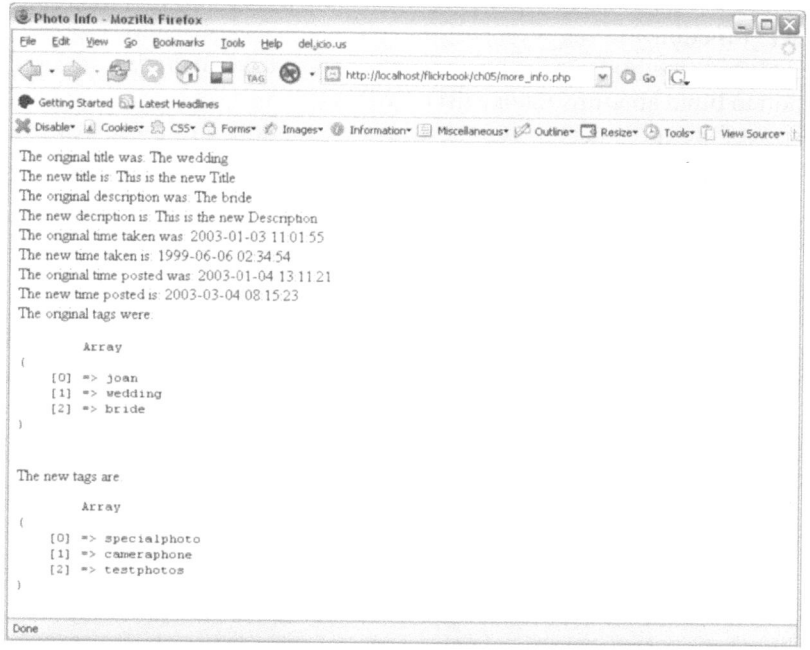

Figure 5-3. *Setting and getting information about a photo*

How It Works

In this example we include the `Phlickr_AuthedPhoto` class instead of the `Phlickr_Photo` class.

```
include_once 'Phlickr/AuthedPhoto.php';
```

Since `Phlickr_AuthedPhoto` is a child class of `Phlickr_Photo`, it inherits all of the methods from `Phlickr_Photo`. We make use of these when we are getting information about the photo.

```
$original_title = $p->getTitle();
$original_description = $p->getDescription();
$original_posted_time = $p->getPostedDate();
$original_taken_time = $p->getTakenDate();
$original_tags = $p->getTags();
```

Then, we use the methods that are specific to `Phlickr_AuthedPhoto` to write information to the photo.

```
$p->setMeta('This is the new Title', 'This is the new Description');
$p->setPosted(mktime (8,15,23,3,4,03));
$p->setTaken(mktime (2,34,54,6,6,99));
$p->setTags(array('specialphoto','cameraphone', 'testphotos'));
```

Here we've used the `setMeta()` method to write a new title and description, `setPosted()` and `setTaken()` to change the times on the photo, and `setTags()` to change the tags on the photo.

Notice that we used the `mktime()` function of PHP to set the time. `mktime()` takes the hour, minute, second, month, date, and year as its arguments and returns a Unix timestamp. Since the `setPosted()` and `setTaken()` methods accept only a timestamp as their argument, it's necessary to use the `mktime()` function.

Similarly, for the `setTags()` method, we need to pass an array of tags. To do this, we used the PHP `array()` function to build an array out of a list of words.

Finally, notice the use of the `<pre>` tag to wrap the array information. This preserves any white space and line breaks that may occur in the output of `print_r()`, so we can see the array structure better.

Summary

In this chapter we've introduced working with the Flickr API using the PHP Phlickr library. We used the `Phlickr_Photo` class to create a simple web page that displays a photo and took a look at all of the methods of the `Phlickr_Photo` class. We've also looked at the `Phlickr_AuthedPhoto` class and used it to change the metadata for a photo. In the following chapters, we'll build on these basic techniques to take advantage of the full Flickr API. In the next chapter, we'll find out how to take the classes and methods we've used in this chapter and apply them to a whole set of photos.

CHAPTER 6

■ ■ ■

Getting Organized: Working with Flickr Photo Sets

Now that you know the ins and outs of how the `Phlickr_Photo` object works, you'll want to start grouping photos together into sets. Flickr sets provide a great mechanism to manage and to arrange your photos so you can present them to viewers through your own website. In this chapter we'll show you how to do just that—use Flickr sets for a back end for your photo site.

Photo Set Basics

To begin with, let's look at the basics of manipulating a photo set.

Try It Out: Creating a Photo Set

In order to create a set, you need to start with at least one existing photo. For this example, we start with a sample photo ID from one of the photos in our account.

```php
<?php
//create_photoset.php

// for the sake of simplicity, we will start with a known photo ID...
// this could be the ID number of any photo in "your photos"
$samplePhotoId = '69368095';

// use the GetToken.php script to generate a config file
define('API_CONFIG_FILE', './authtoken.dat');

// require the needed Phlickr libraries
require_once 'Phlickr/Api.php';
require_once 'Phlickr/AuthedPhotosetList.php';

// set up the api connection
$api = Phlickr_Api::createFrom(API_CONFIG_FILE);

if (! $api->isAuthValid()) {
    die("invalid flickr logon");
}
```

```php
// get the list of photo sets in your account
$photosetlist = new Phlickr_AuthedPhotosetList($api);

// get the id of the newly created photo set
$newphotosetId = $photosetlist->create('the set title', 'the caption', ➥
  $samplePhotoId);

// let's make an object out of the new photo set
$authedPhotoset = new Phlickr_AuthedPhotoset($api, $newphotosetId);

// now let's change the title and description
$authedPhotoset->
  setMeta('this is a better title', 'and this is a better description');

// the URL of the photo set
$url = $authedPhotoset->buildUrl();
?>

<html>
  <head>
    <title>Photoset Basics</title>
  </head>

  <body>
    <p>
      The new photoset id is: <?php echo $newphotosetId; ?><br/>

      The new photoset can be found at:
      <a href="<?php echo $url; ?>"><?php echo $url; ?></a><br/>
    </p>
  </body>
</html>
```

When you open this script in a browser, you will get something that looks like Figure 6-1:

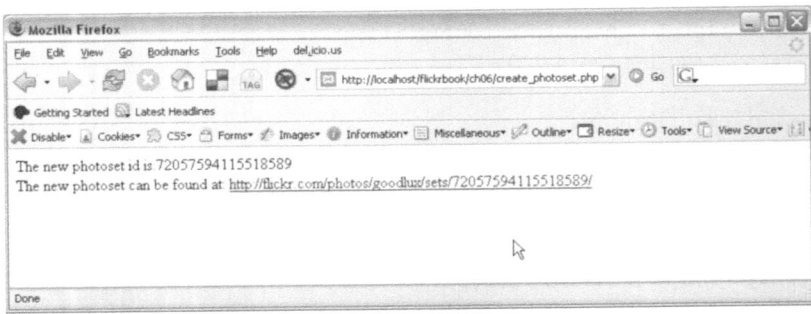

Figure 6-1. *Creating a set*

How It Works

The preceding code is fairly straightforward, given the comments. We start with the ID of a particular photo from our account. When using this example, you will have to use a photo ID from one of the photos in your account. We then include the Phlickr libraries we will need and create an API connection. From there, we grab the list of all the existing photo sets in the account. We append a new photo set to the list using the create() method of AuthedPhotosetList. This method returns the ID of the newly created set. Since our title is a little boring, we use this ID to create a new set and use the setMeta() method to change the set title and caption. Finally, we echo the URL of the new set, which we obtained with the buildUrl() method, to the browser so it can be viewed.

Tags and Sorting

Now that we've looked at the basics of creating and manipulating a set, let's try something a little more involved. This time we'll use tags to create the photo set and sort it.

Try It Out: Creating a Set of Color-Sorted Images from Tags

In the following example, we create a set out of all the photos in your account with a particular tag and have the results sorted by color.

```php
<?php
//sorted_set.php

$tags = $_REQUEST['tags'];

if ($tags != ''){

  // use the GetToken.php script to generate a config file.
  define('API_CONFIG_FILE', './authtoken.dat');

  include_once 'Phlickr/Api.php';
  include_once 'Phlickr/AuthedPhotosetList.php';
  include_once 'Phlickr/PhotoList.php';
  include_once 'Phlickr/PhotoListIterator.php';
  include_once 'Phlickr/PhotoSorter.php';
  include_once 'Phlickr/PhotoSortStrategy/ByColor.php';

  // set up the api connection
  $api = Phlickr_Api::createFrom(API_CONFIG_FILE);
  if (! $api->isAuthValid()) {
    die('invalid flickr logon');
  }
```

```php
$request = $api->createRequest(
  'flickr.photos.search',
  array(
    'tags' => $tags,
    'tag_mode' => 'all',
    'user_id' => $api->getUserId()
  )
);

$pl = new Phlickr_PhotoList($request, Phlickr_PhotoList::PER_PAGE_MAX);
$count = $pl->getCount();

if ($count == 0) {
  print "No photos could be found tagged with $tags.<br/>";
} else {
  print "Found $count photos tagged with $tags...<br/>";

  // create a sorter that will use the color sort strategy
  $strategy = new Phlickr_PhotoSortStrategy_ByColor($api->getCache());
  $sorter = new Phlickr_PhotoSorter($strategy);

  // use a photolist iterator so that all the pages are sorted
  // sorting the photos by color might take a while
  flush();
  $photos = $sorter->sort(new Phlickr_PhotoListIterator($pl));
  $photo_ids = Phlickr_PhotoSorter::idsFromPhotos($photos);

  // create the authed photo set list for the current user...
  $apsl = new Phlickr_AuthedPhotosetList($api);
  // .. and create a new photo set
  $id = $apsl->
    create($tags, 'photo set created from tags ' . $tags, $photo_ids[0]);

  // wait a few seconds for the set to be created
  sleep(3);

  // now, create the photo set object and add the photos
  $aps = new Phlickr_AuthedPhotoset($api, $id);
  $aps->editPhotos($photo_ids[0], $photo_ids);

  $url = $aps->buildUrl();
?>

  Created a photoset named '<?php echo $tags; ?>': <br/>
  <a href='<?php echo $url; ?>'><?php echo $url; ?></a><br/>
```

```php
<?php
  }
} // closing the two if blocks
?>

<html>
  <head>
    <title>Create a sorted set</title>
  </head>

  <body>
    <form method='post' action='sorted_set.php'>
      <p>enter a list of tags <input type='text' name='tags'/></p>
      <input type='submit' value='submit'/>
    </form>

  </body>
</html>
```

When you open this script in a browser window (see Figure 6-2), you will be asked to enter a set of tags that will be used to pull photos for your new set.

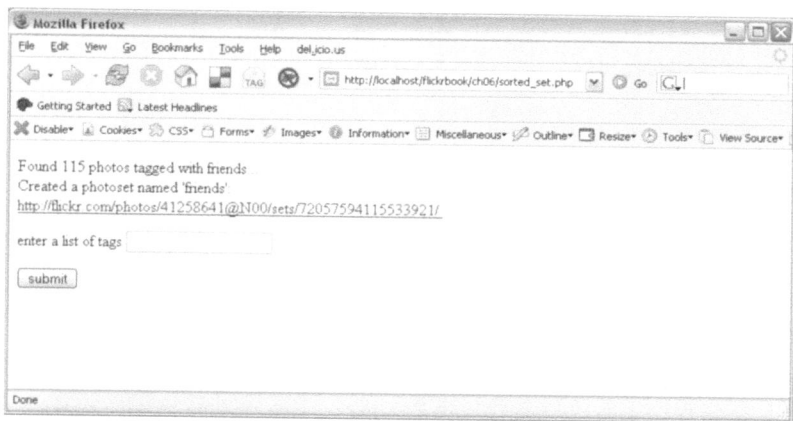

Figure 6-2. *Creating a sorted set*

How It Works

This script begins by setting the $tags variable to the value stored in the special PHP $_REQUEST variable. This variable is called a superglobal, or automatic global, and it's available in any PHP script. The $_REQUEST variable is just one of several superglobal variables. Its purpose is to store the information provided through HTML forms or cookies. In this example, it's used to provide our script with the tag information that is passed to the script through the form at the end of the script. We'll take another look at this when we look at the HTML form at the end of this section. For now it's enough to know that it will be storing a list of user-supplied tags. If there are no user-supplied tags, the whole script is ignored.

The next few lines of code provide a pointer to the authentication information that we will need to connect to Flickr.

```
// use the GetToken.php script to generate a config file.
define('API_CONFIG_FILE', './authtoken.dat');
```

Next, we include the specific Phlickr libraries that are needed to run the code. Once that is done we make a connection to the API using the createFrom() method of the Phlickr_Api object. We also set the API cache to point to the local file that we defined earlier.

```
$api = Phlickr_Api::createFrom(API_CONFIG_FILE);
if (! $api->isAuthValid()) {
  die('invalid flickr logon');
}
```

Once the API connection is set up, we use the list of tags to create a tag search request to send to Flickr.

```
$request = $api->createRequest(
    'flickr.photos.search',
    array(
        'tags' => $tags,
        'tag_mode' => 'all',
        'user_id' => $api->getUserId()
    )
);
```

The results are transformed into a Phlickr_PhotoList object, and we count the number of photos in the PhotoList and check to make sure that there are some photos with the tags specified.

```
$pl = new Phlickr_PhotoList($request, Phlickr_PhotoList::PER_PAGE_MAX);
$count = $pl->getCount();

if ($count == 0) {
  print "No photos could be found tagged with $tags.<br/>";
} else {
  print "Found $count photos tagged with $tags...<br/>";
```

Once we are sure we have some photos, we decide which way we want to sort them, using the PhotoSortStrategy. In this case, we are sorting the photos by color, so we use the Phlickr_PhotoSortStrategy_ByColor object. We then create a Phlickr_PhotoSorter object using this strategy.

```
// create a sorter that will use the color sort strategy
$strategy = new Phlickr_PhotoSortStrategy_ByColor($api->getCache());
$sorter = new Phlickr_PhotoSorter($strategy);
```

```
// use a photolist iterator so that all the pages are sorted.
// sorting the photos by color might take a while
flush();
$photos = $sorter->sort(new Phlickr_PhotoListIterator($pl));
$photo_ids = Phlickr_PhotoSorter::idsFromPhotos($photos);
```

Next we pull up the list of all the photo sets for the current user using the
Phlickr_AuthedPhotosetList object.

```
// create the authed photo set list for the current user...
$apsl = new Phlickr_AuthedPhotosetList($api);
```

Then we append a new photo set to this list, as we did in the first example.

```
// .. and create a new photo set
$id = $apsl->create($tags, 'photo set created from tags ' . $tags, $photo_ids[0]);
```

Flickr needs a little time to register that a new photo set was created, so we use the PHP
sleep() function to wait 3 seconds:

```
// wait a few seconds for the set to be created
sleep(3);
```

Then we add the images into the Flickr photo set using the Phlickr_AuthedPhotoset object
and return information about our newly created set.

```
// now, create the photo set object and add the photos
$aps = new Phlickr_AuthedPhotoset($api, $id);
$aps->editPhotos($photo_ids[0], $photo_ids);

$url = $aps->buildUrl();
?>


Created a photoset named '<?php echo $tags; ?>': <br/>
<a href='<?php echo $url; ?>'><?php echo $url; ?></a><br/>

<?php
  }
} // closing the two if blocks
?>
```

Finally, you will notice some HTML after the PHP portion of the script.

```
<html>
  <head>
    <title>Create a sorted set</title>
  </head>
```

```
<body>
  <form method='post' action='sorted_set.php'>
    <p>enter a list of tags <input type='text' name='tags'/></p>
    <input type='submit' value='submit'/>
  </form>

</body>
</html>
```

This is the HTML code for the form where you can enter the tags that you want to create the set from. In the beginning of the script we used the PHP $_REQUEST['tags'] variable to get our tags. This is where that information came from, through the POST method of an HTML form. Notice that the text area of the form is named tags.

When you log in to Flickr and check your photos, you will find a new set, named with the tags you supplied. The results will look something like Figure 6-3.

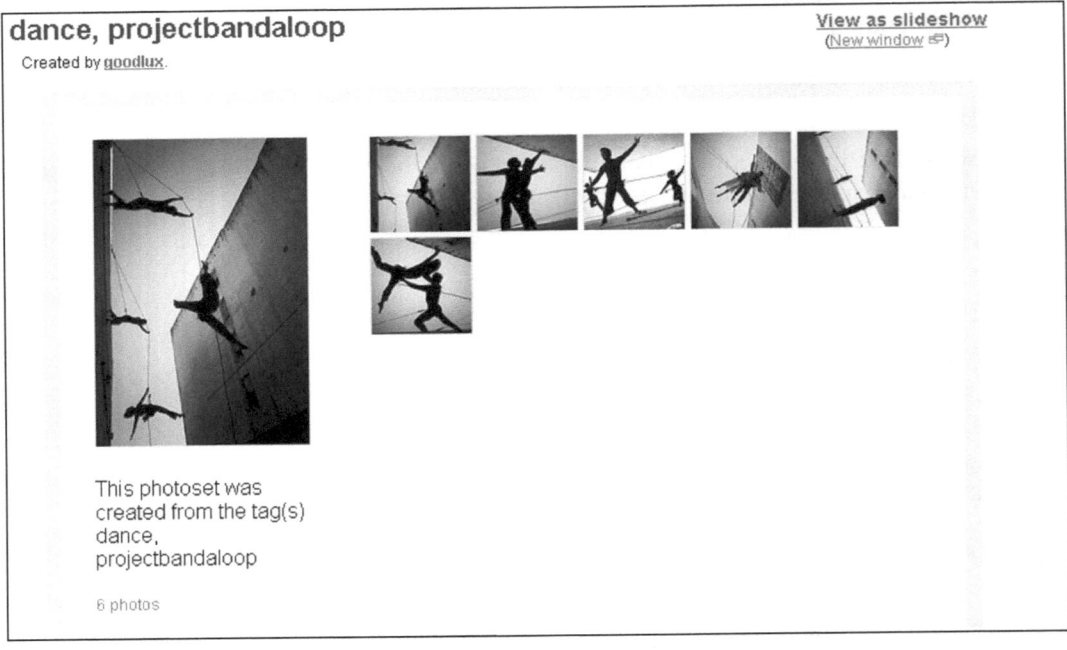

Figure 6-3. *Set created from tags*

One practical use of the color sorting is that it tends to group together photos of a particular individual on a given occasion, because the colors in the person's skin tones and clothing are similar from photo to photo. Try it yourself: run the previous code on your *friends* tag and see what happens!

Displaying a Photo Set on an External Web Page

Flickr is a great back end for managing your photos, but it is limited as a presentation tool. Instead, you might want to show those images in your own personal website in a format that you like. The following two examples demonstrate two ways to display images on your personal web page, using Flickr as the back end.

The first example is a photolog view of a set. This view allows you to leaf through your set, one image at a time, going forward or backward chronologically. The basic photolog view looks something like Figure 6-4.

Figure 6-4. *The photolog view of a set allows you to move through a set in chronological order.*

The second example is a portfolio view of a set. This view shows one large image with several smaller thumbnails below the main photo, as shown in Figure 6-5:

Figure 6-5. *The portfolio view allows you to view one main photo and navigate by thumbnails.*

Both of our examples use two separate pieces of code to run. The first bit of code is a PHP script that connects to Flickr and copies information from the Flickr photo set into a cache file stored on the web server. The second bit of code is a PHP script that reads the data from the cache file and presents the images to the web browser.

The reason we separate these tasks into two distinct pieces of code is to ensure that a person viewing the page can move through the photolog or portfolio quickly. Connecting to Flickr using the API and returning a large set of photos can take several seconds. We wouldn't want the viewer to have to wait that long just to see your latest image. By having one piece of code read through the Flickr photo set and cache the information on the web server, and a second script read the cache and present it to the end user, we can display the images in an acceptable amount of time.

A second advantage of separating these tasks is that it allows you to use the Phlickr libraries to create your website, even if your hosting provider is still using PHP 4. You can run the first script locally on the computer where you've installed PHP 5 and copy the cache file to your web server. The second script does not use the Phlickr PHP 5 libraries, so as long as your host is running PHP 4, it will work fine on your web server.

The main drawback to this approach is that you have to run the first piece of code every time that your Flickr photo set is updated. So if you add new photos to your photolog set on Flickr, you have to run a script to update your website. One easy way to solve this problem is to create a cron job (if you are using the Unix platform) or a scheduled task (on Windows) to run the script at a regular interval. So you could, for instance, have the script run automatically once a day to update your website with any new photos that you've added to your photolog. Or you might want to create a scheduled batch file that both updates your photolog and transmits the cached information using FTP.

Try It Out: Retrieving Photo Information for a Photolog

Let's look at this in practice, with our first example, the photolog view.

```php
<?php
//photolog_cache.php

define('API_CONFIG_FILE', './authtoken.dat');

$serverpath = dirname($_SERVER["SCRIPT_FILENAME"]).'/';

$set = '1205215';

include_once  'Phlickr/Api.php';
include_once  'Phlickr/Photoset.php';

$api = Phlickr_Api::createFrom(API_CONFIG_FILE);

if (! $api->isAuthValid()) {
  die("invalid flickr logon");
}

$ps = new Phlickr_Photoset($api, $set);

$psl = $ps->getPhotoList();

$photos = $psl->getPhotos();

$cache_array = array();
$i = 0;

echo "Creating cache file...<br/>";

foreach ($photos as $photo){

  $cache_array[$i][0] = $photo->buildImgUrl('-');
  $cache_array[$i][1] = $photo->getTitle();
  $cache_array[$i][2] = $photo->getTakenTimestamp();
  $cache_array[$i][3] = $photo->getId();
  echo 'Caching information for '.$cache_array[$i][0]."<br/>";
  flush();
  $i++;

}
```

```
$dat = serialize($cache_array);
$f = file_put_contents("$serverpath$set.dat", $dat);
echo 'Cache file created and stored at '.$serverpath."<br/>";
?>
```

How It Works

In the first part of this example, we create a script that connects to Flickr and copies data into a file that we will use for the second part. To do this, we first set the path to the authentication token that we created in Chapter 3. We also set two variables: the $serverpath, which is the directory that we will copy our file to, and the $set variable, which is the ID of the set that will provide images for the photolog.

Notice that we are again using a PHP superglobal variable. This time it's the $_SERVER superglobal, which provides information directly from the web server. Here we are using it to provide the file name and path of the current script. This information is enclosed in the PHP dirname() function so that only the path information of the current script is returned to the $serverpath variable. This will allow us to store the cached information in the same directory that the script is run from.

Next we include the Phlickr API library and create an API connection as we did in the previous example. Once the connection is created, we can create a new Phlickr_Photoset from the ID we provided.

```
$ps = new Phlickr_Photoset($api, $set);
```

We then assign the photos from the photo set to the variable $photos.

```
$psl = $ps->getPhotoList();
$photos = $psl->getPhotos();
```

Using a foreach loop, we iterate over the photos and store information about each photo in an array, $cache_array. In this case, we get the URL of the photo, the title, and the time the photo was taken, as well as the ID of the photo.

When the loop completes, we make our array permanent using the PHP serialize() function and save the results into a file on the web server using the file_put_contents() function. In this case, it saves the file as 1205215.dat, which is the ID of our set with a .dat extension. You could pick a different file name or extension if you like.

Try It Out: Displaying Photos in a Photolog

So we now have a compact data file on our web server that we can use in our second script to rapidly access that information. In the next step, we will access the cache file from a web page and use the cached information to present our Flickr images on our website.

```
<?php
//photolog_view.php

$photolog_set_id = '1205215';
$pageurl = $_SERVER["SCRIPT_NAME"].'/';
$flickr_username = "goodlux";
```

```php
$key = 0;

$path_array = explode("/",$_SERVER["PATH_INFO"]);
$mainPhotoId = $path_array[1];

$filename = dirname($_SERVER["SCRIPT_FILENAME"]).'/'."$photolog_set_id.dat";
$cache = file_get_contents($filename);

$photos = unserialize($cache);
$num_photos = count($photos);

if (($mainPhotoId == NULL)|| (!isset($mainPhotoId))) {
  $mainPhotoId = $photos[0][3];
}

while ($photos[$key][3] != $mainPhotoId) {
  $key++;
}


if (($photos[$key][1] == NULL)) {
  $title = 'Click to view';
} else {
  $title = $photos[$key][1];
}

$photodate = date( "l, M jS Y" ,$photos[$key][2]);

$now_url = $pageurl.$photos[$key-1][3].'/';
$then_url = $pageurl.$photos[$key+1][3].'/';

if ($key <= 4) {
  $then5_url = $pageurl.$photos[$key+5][3].'/';
  $now5_url = $pageurl.$photos[0][3].'/';
} elseif ($key >= $num_photos-5) {
  $then5_url = $pageurl.$photos[$num_photos-1][3].'/';
  $now5_url = $pageurl.$photos[$key-5][3].'/';
} else {
  $then5_url = $pageurl.$photos[$key+5][3].'/';
  $now5_url = $pageurl.$photos[$key-5][3].'/';
}
?>

<html>
  <head>
    <title>Photolog Viewer</title>
  </head>
```

```php
<body>
  <div align='center'>

    <table>
      <tr valign='bottom' height='25'>
        <td align='center'>
          <h3><?php echo $photodate; ?></h3>
        </td>
      </tr>
      <tr>
        <td>
          <table>

            <?php
            if ($photos[$key-1][3] == '') { //newest photo
            ?>
            <tr valign='top' align='center'>
              <td align='right' width='30'>
                <a href='<?php echo $then5_url; ?>' title='rewind'>&#60;&#60;</a>
              </td>
              <td align='right' width='42'>
                <a href='<?php echo $then_url; ?>'
                   title='previous photo'>&#60;then</a>
              </td>
              <td width='520' align='center'>
                <img class='main' src='<?php echo $photos[$key][0]; ?>' ALT='*' />
              </td>
              <td align='left' width='38'/>
              <td width='30'/>
            </tr>

            <?php
            } elseif ($photos[$key+1][3] == '') { //oldest photo
            ?>
            <tr valign='top'>
              <td align='right' width='30'/>
              <td align='right' width='42'/>
              <td width='520' align='center'>
                <img class='main' src='<?php echo $photos[$key][0]; ?>' ALT='*' />
              </td>
              <td width='38' align='left'>
                <a href='<?php echo $now_url; ?>' title='next photo'>now&#62;</a>
              </td>
              <td align='left' width='30'>
                <a href='<?php echo $now5_url; ?>'
                   title='fastforward'>&#62;&#62;</a>
              </td>
            </tr>
```

```php
<?php
} else { //everything else
?>
<tr  valign='top'>
  <td align='right' width='30'>
    <a href='<?php echo $then5_url; ?>' title='rewind'>&#60;&#60;</a>
  </td>
  <td align='right' width='42'>
    <a href='<?php echo $then_url; ?>'
       title='previous photo'>&#60;then</a>
  </td>
  <td width='520' align='center'>
    <img class='main' src='<?php echo $photos[$key][0]; ?>' ALT='*' />
  </td>
  <td align='left' width='38'>
    <a href='<?php echo $now_url; ?>' title='next photo'>now&#62;</a>
  </td>
  <td align='left' width='30'>
    <a href='<?php echo $now5_url; ?>'
       title='fastforward'>&#62;&#62;</a>
  </td>
</tr>

<?php
} // close the if block

// create a URL
$url = 'http://www.flickr.com/photos/' ➥
  .$flickr_username.'/'.$photos[$key][3];
?>

    </table>
  </td>
</tr>
</table>

<table>
  <tr valign='top'>
    <td align='center'  height='20'>
      <a href='<?php echo $url; ?>'><?php echo $title; ?></a>
    </td>
  </tr>
</table>

    </div>
  </body>
</html>
```

How It Works

The second part of our example is a PHP script that that grabs information from our cache file and uses it to display a web page to the user.

In order to use PHP to create the HTML to display our photolog (Figure 6-4), we need a few pieces of information. First we need the ID of the image that will be displayed. We also need the ID of the previous image and the next image to create the forward and backward links. Additionally, to make our photolog more interesting, we added the ability to jump forward or backwards five images, so we need the IDs of the images five before and after our current image.

There is one caveat here. If the current image is the newest image, we don't want to see the forward links, since those images don't exist yet. Similarly, if the current image is the oldest image, we don't want to see the previous links, because there aren't any older images in our photolog.

Here's how it works. We store the ID of the main photo that we want to display in the URL. If there is no number stored in the URL, the script assumes that you are looking at the newest image in the photolog, and the script uses the ID of the newest image. We then look up this ID in the cache file we created above. We jump forward and back one image and store those IDs also, as well as the IDs of the images five places forwards and back.

Let's walk through the code. First we set a few variables. $photolog_set_id is the ID of the set we used in the first part of our example. This is used only to get the file name that we stored the serialized array data in. $pageurl stores the URL of the HTML page that the script is running in. This makes creating the HTML links more convenient. The $flickr_username variable is the username (or ID) of the user whose photos we are using for the photolog. We also initialize the $key variable that will be used as a pointer to keep track of our position in the array.

Next, we use the PHP explode() function to break the current URL into pieces, and we store the pieces in the $path_array variable. The piece of information that we are interested is the second piece of information, the photo ID, stored in $path_array[1].

```
$path_array = explode("/",$_SERVER["PATH_INFO"]);
$mainPhotoId = $path_array[1];
```

Remember that if there is no photo ID in the URL, the script assumes that you are looking at the newest image in the photo set. In this case $mainPhotoId is null.

The next step is to open up our file with the cached data and to create an array from it using the unserialize() function.

```
$filename = dirname($_SERVER["SCRIPT_FILENAME"]).'/'."$photolog_set_id.dat";
$cache = file_get_contents($filename);

$photos = unserialize($dat);
```

We can then access the data and count the number of photos in the set.

```
$num_photos = count($photos);
```

Also, if $mainPhotoId is NULL because there was no ID passed in the URL, we can get the ID of the newest image in the set and use that for the $mainPhotoId.

```
if (($mainPhotoId == NULL)|| (!isset($mainPhotoId))) {
  $mainPhotoId = $photos[0][3];
}
```

Now that we have a $mainPhotoId, we cycle through the $photo array until we find the array key of that stored ID.

```
while ($photos[$key][3] != $mainPhotoId) {
  $key++;
}
```

Then we find the title of that particular photo and store it in the $title variable. If the photo has no title we use the HTML $nbsp; character to leave blank space.

```
if (($photos[$key][1] == NULL)) {
  $title = 'Click to view';
} else {
  $title = $photos[$key][1];
}
```

We also grab out of the array the date the photo was taken on and format it.

```
$photodate = date( "l, M jS Y" ,$photos[$key][2]);
```

Next we create URLs containing the previous and next photo IDs.

```
$now_url = $pageurl.$photos[$key-1][3].'/';
$then_url = $pageurl.$photos[$key+1][3].'/';
```

To get the IDs of the images five places backwards or forwards from the current image, we do some if/then/else kung fu. This is a little tricky. Say, for instance, that we are displaying the third image from the newest. If we hop ahead five images, we've gone out of range; there are only three images ahead. In that case, we want to use the ID of the image three images ahead, not five. The following code accomplishes this, storing the appropriate URLs in the $then5_url and the $now5_url variables.

```
if ($key <= 4) {
  $then5_url = $pageurl.$photos[$key+5][3].'/';
  $now5_url = $pageurl.$photos[0][3].'/';
} elseif ($key >= $num_photos-5) {
  $then5_url = $pageurl.$photos[$num_photos-1][3].'/';
  $now5_url = $pageurl.$photos[$key-5][3].'/';
} else {
  $then5_url = $pageurl.$photos[$key+5][3].'/';
  $now5_url = $pageurl.$photos[$key-5][3].'/';
}
```

Now we have everything we need to draw up the page. To make our photolog look nice, we put everything into a table. We draw the top of the table with the following HTML:

```
<html>
  <head>
    <title>Photolog Viewer</title>
  </head>

  <body>
    <div align='center'>

      <table>
        <tr valign='bottom' height='25'>
          <td align='center'>
            <h3><?php echo $photodate; ?></h3>
          </td>
        </tr>
        <tr>
          <td>
            <table>
```

Next we have to make some decisions. If this is the newest image in the set, we don't want to show the forward links. If it is the oldest, we don't want to show the back links. Otherwise, we want to show both links. Using the if/elseif/else conditional statement, we echo the appropriate HTML code.

```
if ($photos[$key-1][3]=='') { //newest photo
...
} elseif ($photos[$key+1][3]=='') { //oldest photo
...
} else { //everything else
...
} // close the if block
```

Finally, for effect, we link the title back to the actual photo page on Flickr and close off the table. You will have to set the $flickr_username variable to your Flickr user name if you want to use your own photos.

```
      // create a URL
      $url = 'http://www.flickr.com/photos/'
       .$flickr_username.'/'.$photos[$key][3];
      ?>

          </table>
        </td>
      </tr>
    </table>
```

```
    <table>
      <tr valign='top'>
        <td align='center' height='20'>
          <a href='<?php echo $url; ?>'><?php echo $title; ?></a>
        </td>
      </tr>
    </table>

  </div>
 </body>
</html>
```

Voila! There you have it, a whole photolog in a single web page. Notice that all of the images in this example are actually stored on Flickr, but they are displayed in your web page. This is a great way to save space on your web server. This works well when you are looking at one image at a time. However, when you are looking at several images at once, there can be a time lag while the images load from the Flickr servers.

Try It Out: Retrieving Photos for a Portfolio

In the next example, in addition to caching information from the set, we cache the image files on the web server. Let's take a look.

```php
<?php
//portfolio_cache.php

define('API_CONFIG_FILE', '../authtoken.dat');

include_once 'Phlickr/Api.php';
include_once 'Phlickr/Photoset.php';

$serverpath = dirname($_SERVER["SCRIPT_FILENAME"]).'/';
$webpath = '';

$set = '216005';

$cache_arraypi = Phlickr_Api::createFrom(API_CONFIG_FILE);
if (! $cache_arraypi->isAuthValid()) {
  die("invalid flickr logon");
}

$ps = new Phlickr_Photoset($cache_arraypi, $set);
$psl = $ps->getPhotoList();
$photos = $psl->getPhotos();

$cache_array = array();
$i = 0;
```

```php
echo "Creating cache file and downloading images...<br/>";
foreach ($photos as $photo){
  if ($i<15) {
    $url1 = $photo->buildImgUrl('-');
    $url2 = $photo->buildImgUrl('s');

    $pu1 = parse_url($url1);
    $pu2 = parse_url($url2);

    $url1_path = $pu1['path'];
    $url2_path = $pu2['path'];

    $pi1 = pathinfo($url1_path);
    $pi2 = pathinfo($url2_path);

    $filename1 = $pi1['basename'];
    $filename2 = $pi2['basename'];

    $cache_array[$i][0] = $webpath.$filename1;
    $cache_array[$i][1] = $webpath.$filename2;
    $cache_array[$i][2] = $photo->getTitle();

    $img1 = file_get_contents($url1);
    $img2 = file_get_contents($url2);

    file_put_contents($serverpath.$filename1, $img1);
    file_put_contents($serverpath.$filename2, $img2);
    echo "Saved ".$serverpath.$filename1."<br/>";
    flush();
  }

  $i++;
}

$dat = serialize($cache_array);
file_put_contents($serverpath."$set.dat", $dat);
echo "Cache file created and stored at $serverpath<br/>";
?>
```

When you view this page in a browser, you should see something that looks similar to Figure 6-6.

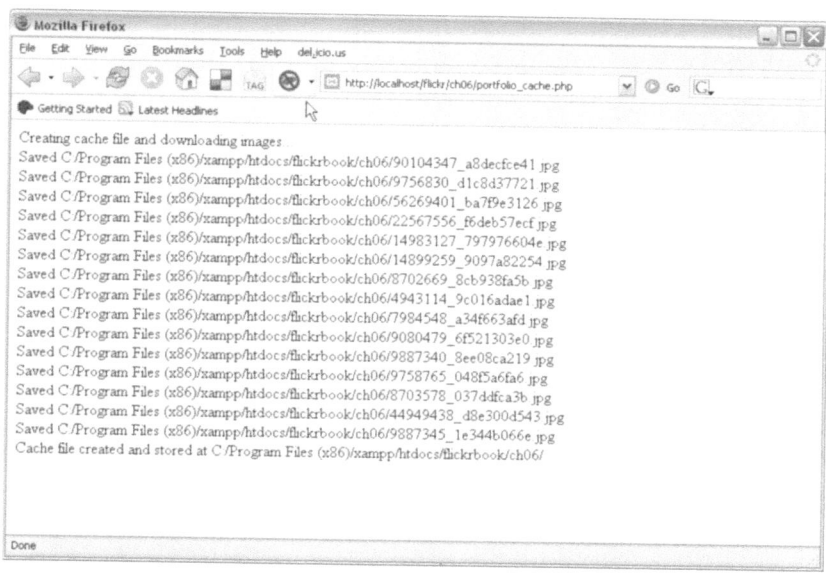

Figure 6-6. *Creating the portfolio cache*

How It Works

In many ways, this example is similar to the previous one. Here we are creating an API connection using the authentication token and the Phlickr API library, and storing information about the set in an array that we serialize and save to the web server. The main difference is that we copy the image, both in its square thumbnail size and its regular size. So in this example, for each image, there are two files that we copy to our web server:

```
$ps = new Phlickr_Photoset($api, $set);
$psl = $ps->getPhotoList();
$photos = $psl->getPhotos();
```

We then iterate over the list of images, looking at the first 15 images in the set, using a foreach loop:

```
foreach ($photos as $photo){
  if ($i<15) {
```

For each of the 15 photos, we get the URL of both the regular-size image and the thumbnail.

```
$url1 = $photo->buildImgUrl('-');
$url2 = $photo->buildImgUrl('s');
```

From these URLs we extract the file name and path to the image on the Flickr server.

```
$pu1 = parse_url($url1);
$pu2 = parse_url($url2);
```

```
$url1_path = $pu1['path'];
$url2_path = $pu2['path'];

$pi1 = pathinfo($url1_path);
$pi2 = pathinfo($url2_path);

$filename1 = $pi1['basename'];
$filename2 = $pi2['basename'];
```

Then we save in our array the location where the downloaded file will be stored on the local server, as well as the title of the image.

```
$cache_array[$i][0] = $webpath.$filename1;
$cache_array[$i][1] = $webpath.$filename2;
$cache_array[$i][2] = $photo->getTitle();
```

We grab and save the image files using the file_get_contents() and file_put_contents() functions. When we have done this for all of our photos, we save the array of information to a file.

```
$dat = serialize($cache_array);
file_put_contents($serverpath."$set.dat", $dat);
```

Try It Out: Displaying Photos in a Portfolio

So now we have the images, the thumbnails, and an array with information about the files and their location stored on the web server. The next step is to take this information and present it as HTML.

```
<?php
//portfolio_view.php

$setid = '216005';

$filename = dirname($_SERVER["SCRIPT_FILENAME"])."/$setid.dat";
$dat = file_get_contents($filename);
$photos = unserialize($dat);

$num_photos = count($photos);
if ($num_photos > 15) {
  $num_photos = 15;
}

$path_array = explode("/", $_SERVER["PATH_INFO"]);
$mainPhotoId = $path_array[2];

if (($mainPhotoId == NULL )|| (!isset($mainPhotoId))) {
  $mainPhotoId = 0;
}
```

```php
if (($photos[$mainPhotoId][2] == NULL)) {
  $title = ' ';
}else{
  $title = $photos[$mainPhotoId][2];
}

$currentFile = $_SERVER["SCRIPT_NAME"];
$baseUrl = 'http://localhost'.$currentFile.'/'.$setid.'/';
$dirName = dirname($currentFile);
?>

<html>
  <head>
    <title>Portfolio View</title>
  </head>

  <body>

    <table width="1000" align="center">
      <tr valign="top">
        <td width="885" align="center" valign="top" >
          <table cellpadding="25" align="center">
            <tr align='center'>
              <td>
              </td>
            </tr>
          </table>
          <table cellpadding='0' cellspacing='0' width='100%'>
            <tr halign='middle' valign='center'>
              <td align='center' height='650'>
                <img src='<?php echo $dirName.'/'.$photos[$mainPhotoId][0]; ?>'
                    ALT='*' />
              </td>
            </tr>
            <tr valign='top'>
              <td align='center' height='20'>
                <h3><?php echo $title; ?></h3>
              </td>
            </tr>
          </table>

          <table height='52'>
            <tr>
```

```php
            <?php
            for ($i = 0; $i< $num_photos; $i++){
            ?>
              <td>
                <a href="<?php echo $baseUrl.$i; ?>">
                  <img border="0" height="30" width="30"
                       src="<?php echo $dirName.'/'.$photos[$i][1]; ?>">
                </a>
              </td>
            <?php
            }
            ?>

            </tr>
          </table>
        </td>
      </tr>
    </table>
  </body>
</html>
```

How It Works

In this example, the presentation is a little bit less complicated than in the last. All we really need to know is which photo needs to be displayed, and the locations and file names of the thumbnails and other files. It isn't important to know which order the files are in, or which comes previous or next to the current image, since the user is free to click on any of the thumbnails to view the larger image. We'll also limit it to 15 images.

We accomplish this in much the same manner as the previous example. The ID of the main photo is stored in the URL. If the URL doesn't have an ID, it automatically shows the first image.

Our first step is to open and unserialize the images' cached data.

```php
$setid = '216005';

$filename = dirname($_SERVER["SCRIPT_FILENAME"])."/$setid.dat";
$dat = file_get_contents($filename);
$photos = unserialize($dat);

$num_photos = count($photos);
if ($num_photos > 15) {
  $num_photos = 15;
}
```

We then check to see if there is an ID in the current URL. If there isn't, we assign the first ID in the set to the $mainPhotoId array.

```php
$path_array = explode("/", $_SERVER["PATH_INFO"]);
$mainPhotoId = $path_array[2];
```

```
if (($mainPhotoId == NULL)|| (!isset($mainPhotoId))) {
  $mainPhotoId = 0;
}
```

Then we store the title of the image in the $title variable. If the photo has no title, we use the HTML   blank space character as a placeholder.

```
if (($photos[$mainPhotoId][2] == NULL)) {
  $title = ' ';
}else{
  $title = $photos[$mainPhotoId][2];
}
```

We set the $currentFile variable to the file name of the code that the script is running from and build the base URL using this value and the set's ID. We'll use this in the photo thumbnails. We also need the path to the file so that the server displays the images correctly, no matter where our file and photos are on the web server. For example, the $currentFile setting for this file is /flickrbook/ch06/portfolio_view.php, so $dirName is /flickrbook/ch06. Now we don't have to worry about the path to the images, because we can automatically calculate it.

This is important, because placing the ID in the URL affects the context that the web server uses, depending on its settings. For example, viewing the image with portfolio_view.php/216005/7 makes /flickrbook/ch06/portfolio_view.php/216005/7 the current directory, rather than /flickrbook/ch06, with the result that the images won't be displayed if the link to them points to the current directory.

```
$currentFile = $_SERVER["SCRIPT_NAME"];
$baseUrl = 'http://localhost'.$currentFile.'/'.$setid.'/';
$dirName = dirname($currentFile);
?>
```

Next, we break out of our PHP code and use some standard HTML to set up the format of the page and tables that will display the images.

```
<html>
  <head>
    <title>Portfolio View</title>
  </head>

  <body>

    <table width="1000" align="center">
      <tr valign="top">
        <td width="885" align="center" valign="top" >
          <table cellpadding="25" align="center">
            <tr align='center'>
              <td>
              </td>
            </tr>
          </table>
```

Following is the HTML that will display our main photo page. Notice the PHP code that is interspersed in the code to display information about our photo. The PHP to display the photo itself uses the $dirName variable to indicate the path to the image.

```
<table cellpadding='0' cellspacing='0' width='100%'>
  <tr halign='middle' valign='center'>
    <td align='center' height='650'>
      <img src='<?php echo $dirName.'/'.$photos[$mainPhotoId][0]; ?>'
           ALT='*' />
    </td>
  </tr>
  <tr valign='top'>
    <td align='center' height='20'>
      <h3><?php echo $title; ?></h3>
    </td>
  </tr>
</table>

<table height='52'>
  <tr>
```

Then we use a for loop to cycle through all of the images and place the thumbnails on the screen. Here again you can see where we use the $dirName variable to add the path to the images. Notice how we build the link to the main photo with the $baseUrl variable:

```
<?php
for ($i = 0; $i< $num_photos; $i++){
?>
  <td>
    <a href="<?php echo $baseUrl.$i; ?>">
      <img border="0" height="30" width="30"
           src="<?php echo $dirName.'/'.$photos[$i][1]; ?>">
    </a>
  </td>
<?php
}
?>
```

Finally, we add in the final HTML tags to close off the tables and the page.

```
          </tr>
        </table>
      </td>
    </tr>
  </table>
  </body>
</html>
```

Now we have a page that displays a main image with 15 thumbnail images below it. When you click on a thumbnail, the page brings that image up as the main image. The response time is very quick, since all of the files are stored on the web server, rather than referencing files that are stored on Flickr's server. As an additional bonus, there is no need to link back to Flickr (unless you want to), as you are not violating the Flickr terms of service since you are storing the images on your website.

Summary

In this chapter we showed you the basics of creating sets using the Phlickr PHP library and expanded on the basics. We created a set that is sorted by color, then showed you two ways to display images stored in a Flickr photo set on an external server. In the next chapter we'll show you how to take advantage of another way of categorizing and grouping photos: tags.

■ ■ ■

Semantic Tags and What They Mean to You: Programming with Flickr Tags

By now you've probably realized the flexibility and utility that tagging brings to managing your photos. In this chapter we'll work exclusively with tags and see some of the ways you can use the API to access stored tags and put them to use. Before we do so, however, we'll look over how to work with the XML that comes back from Flickr.

XML Overview

Before getting into SimpleXML, PHP's extension for working with XML, we'll discuss the basics and nomenclature of XML. If you're already familiar with it, feel free to skip to the next section.

XML stands for eXtensible Markup Language. Put simply, it's a standard for representing many different kinds of data in a structured text format. If you've worked with HTML, the format of XML will look familiar.

```
<?xml version="1.0" encoding="UTF-8"?>
<receipt total="4.26" date="2006-02-01">
  <item cost="2.99">Mocha</item>
  <item cost="1.00">Coffee</item>
  <tax cost="0.27" />
</receipt>
```

The first line is the declaration that describes which version of XML is being used and the encoding. The rest is made up of elements, attributes, and contents.

XML uses pairs of tags called *elements* to structure data. Elements consist of a *start tag* and an *end tag*. The start tag consists of a name surrounded by angle brackets: `<element>`. The end tag is identical, except the name is preceded by a forward slash: `</element>`.

Any text or nested elements between the start and end tags are known as the element's *contents*. An element with no contents, like `<element></element>`, can be represented using the *empty element tag* (`<element />`).

Each element may have multiple name-value pairs known as *attributes*. Attributes are written in the form `name`, followed by the equals sign, followed by the value in quotes: `name="value"`.

In the preceding XML there are three elements: receipt, item, and tax. The receipt element is called the root element because it encloses every other element. It has two attributes, total and date. The contents of the receipt element are the two item elements and the tax element. The content of the first item element is Mocha.

SimpleXML

The SimpleXML extension is one of the most exciting new features in PHP 5. As the name implies, by providing a natural PHP interface to XML, it makes reading and manipulating XML data simple. This makes it ideal for tasks like parsing Flickr's feeds and other data returned by the Flickr API. We'll parse sets of tags later in the chapter, but first let's look at an example of parsing other XML data.

Try It Out: Parsing XML

We'll look at a feed for one author's Flickr photos. For now, all we need to know is that Flickr feeds are XML documents that describe a set of photographs. (We'll see more on this in the next chapter.) Here's a simplified version of a feed found at: http://flickr.com/services/feeds/photos_public.gne?ids=26159919@N00,41258641@N00. For clarity and lack of space, a number of unneeded elements have been removed.

```
<?xml version="1.0" encoding="utf-8" standalone="yes"?>
<feed version="0.3" xmlns="http://purl.org/atom/ns#" ➥
  xmlns:dc="http://purl.org/dc/elements/1.1/">
  <title>drewish's and goodlux's Photos</title>
  <info type="text/html" mode="escaped">
    A feed of drewish's and goodlux's Photos
  </info>
  <modified>2005-12-21T07:57:29Z</modified>
  <entry>
    <title>IMG_6335</title>
    <link rel="alternate" type="text/html" ➥
        href="http://www.flickr.com/photos/goodlux/75850172/"/>
    <issued>2005-12-21T07:57:29Z</issued>
    <modified>2005-12-21T07:57:29Z</modified>
    <author>
      <name>goodlux</name>
      <url>http://www.flickr.com/people/goodlux/</url>
    </author>
    <dc:subject>atlieremmanuel</dc:subject>
  </entry>
  <entry>
    <title>kung fu drea</title>
    <link rel="alternate" type="text/html" ➥
        href="http://www.flickr.com/photos/drewish/75379969/"/>
    <issued>2005-12-20T00:19:56Z</issued>
    <modified>2005-12-20T00:19:56Z</modified>
```

```
    <author>
      <name>drewish</name>
      <url>http://www.flickr.com/people/drewish/</url>
    </author>
    <dc:subject>
      lomo roll26 portland oregon person kungfu drea blueflash
    </dc:subject>
  </entry>
</feed>
```

Following is an example that will retrieve the feed from that URL and print out the feed's title and then the title and URL for each photo listed in the feed:

```php
<?php
// parse_xml.php

$url = ➥
 'http://flickr.com/services/feeds/photos_public.gne?ids=26159919@N00,41258641@N00';
$feed = simplexml_load_file(rawurlencode($url));
?>

<html>
  <head>
    <title>Parsing an XML file</title>
  </head>

  <body>
    <h1><?php echo $feed->title; ?></h1>


    <?php
    foreach ($feed->entry as $entry) {
    ?>

    <a href="<?php echo $entry->link['href']; ?>">
      <?php echo $entry->title; ?></a><br/>

    <?php
    }
    ?>
  </body>
</html>
```

How It Works

If we had wanted to create the SimpleXML object from a string, `simplexml_load_string()` would do the job. In this example, we used `simplexml_load_file()` to create the SimpleXML object. As the example demonstrates, the file doesn't need to be a file local to your computer;

it can be a remote file on a website. PHP handles the busy work of connecting to Flickr's web server, downloading the feed, and loading it into a string.

Note There is one caveat to using `simplexml_load_file()` in PHP 5.0.x. The underlying library, `libxml2`, unescapes the URL, so if you're passing multiple parameters, you'll need to work around it: `simplexml_load_file(rawurlencode('http://flickr.com/?a='. urlencode('b&c')));`. In PHP 5.1.0 and later, you don't need to worry about this; PHP takes care of it for you.

The child elements of the SimpleXML object are accessed using the -> operator. To access the <title> element that is enclosed by the <feed> element in the example feed, we would use `$feed->title`. (<title> is referred to as the child element of <feed>, and <feed> is referred to as the parent element of <title>.) If you refer back to the original XML, the document's root element is <feed>, giving us a logical choice for the variable name.

Multiple elements of the same name are put into an array. In the example, we used the `foreach` statement to iterate through the <entry> elements stored in the array `$feed->entry`. If we had wanted to access only the title of the first photo, we could have instead used `$feed->entry[0]->title`.

Attributes of an element are accessed using the [ ] array syntax. For instance, to access the `href` attribute of first entry's link (`<feed><entry><link href="http...">`), we'd use `$feed->entry[0]->link['href']`.

Now that we know how to work with XML, let's turn our attention to tags.

Accessing Tags

In Chapter 5, we saw how to use the `print_r()` function to print a photo's tags to the screen. This is a great way to get a quick look inside of a tag array, but it isn't very helpful if you actually need to use those tags. So we'll do something more useful.

Try It Out: Iterating Through Tags

Let's start out by simply iterating over a tag array and echoing the tags. (We don't need to work with XML just yet.)

```php
<?php
//tag_sort.php

define('API_CONFIG_FILE', './authtoken.dat');

include_once 'Phlickr/Api.php';
include_once 'Phlickr/Photo.php';

$api = Phlickr_Api::createFrom(API_CONFIG_FILE);
if (! $api->isAuthValid()) {
  die("invalid flickr logon");
}
```

```php
$photo_id = $_REQUEST['photoid'];
$script_filename = basename($_SERVER['SCRIPT_FILENAME']);

?>

<html>
  <head>
    <title>Accessing Tags</title>
  </head>

  <body>
    <form method='post' action='<?php echo $script_filename; ?>'>
      <p>enter a photo id: <input type='text' name='photoid' ➥
          value="<?php echo $photo_id; ?>"/></p>
      <input type='submit' value='find tags for this photo'/>
    </form>

    <?php
    if ($photo_id == NULL) {
      die();
    }

    try {
      $photo = new Phlickr_Photo($api, $photo_id);
      $tags = $photo->getTags();

      if (count($tags) == 0) {
        die("this photo doesn't have any tags");
      }
    ?>

    <br/>
    These are the tags for photo number <?php echo $photo_id; ?>:<br/>

    <?php
      foreach ($tags as $tag) {
        echo $tag."<br/>";
      }
    ?>

    <br/>
    Let's sort the tags<br/>

    <?php
      sort($tags);
```

```php
      foreach ($tags as $tag) {
        echo $tag."<br/>";
      }
  ?>

  <br/>
  Now let's sort them backwards<br/>

  <?php
    rsort($tags);

    foreach ($tags as $tag) {
      echo $tag."<br/>";
    }

  } catch (Exception $e) {
    echo "That doesn't look like a valid photo id. Try again.";
  }
  ?>

</body>
</html>
```

When viewed in a browser window, you will get a form that requests a photo ID. When you submit a valid photo ID, you will get a list of the tags on the photo if there are any, as shown in Figure 7-1.

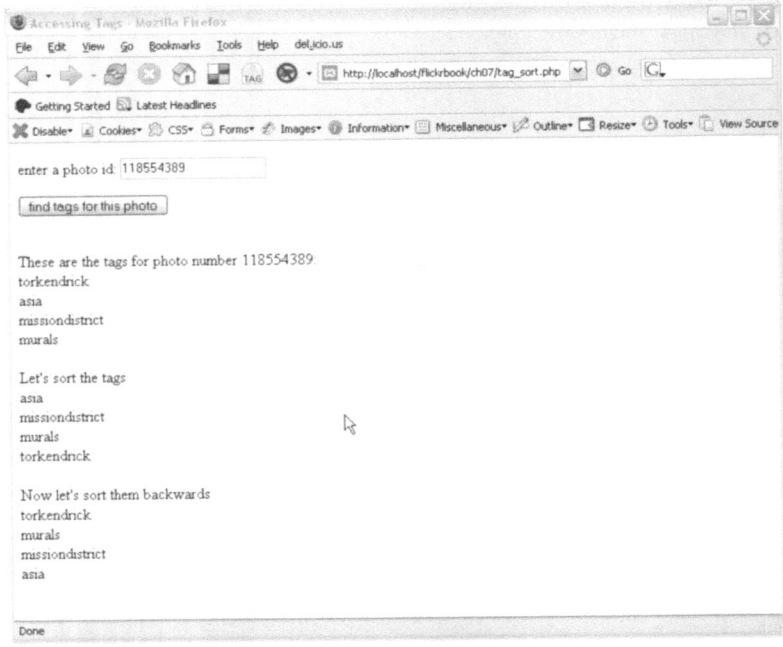

Figure 7-1. *The tags for a photo have been iterated over and sorted.*

How It Works

In this example we use PHP code combined with HTML to produce a simple form page. After we include the necessary files and create an API connection, we set two variables using PHP superglobal variables.

```
$photo_id = $_REQUEST['photoid'];
$script_filename = basename($_SERVER['SCRIPT_FILENAME']);
```

The $photo_id variable is set to whatever ID the user supplies through the form. The $script_filename variable is set to the name of the current file, using the PHP basename() function and the $_SERVER['SCRIPT_FILENAME'] superglobal variable. We then produce the HTML headers and form.

```
<html>
  <head>
    <title>Accessing Tags</title>
  </head>

  <body>
    <form method='post' action='<?php echo $script_filename; ?>'>
      <p>enter a photo id: <input type='text' name='photoid' ➥
          value="<?php echo $photo_id; ?>"/></p>
      <input type='submit' value='find tags for this photo'/>
    </form>
```

Notice how we intersperse the form with PHP inserts, using the $script_filename variable and the $photo_id variable to fill in the appropriate parts of the HTML form. We then jump back to PHP code, checking the $photo_id variable to make sure that it isn't blank.

```
if ($photo_id == NULL){
  die();
}
```

If it is, we don't want to open an API connection or go any further. Next we use a try...catch block to catch errors or exceptions thrown by the request attempt. It could be that the $photo_id that the user has supplied doesn't exist. This would throw an ugly exception if the code were not enclosed in a try block.

Once the programmatic structure is set, we use the getTags() method of the Phlickr_Photo class to return an array of tags, which we store in the $tags variable. We use a foreach loop to go through the tags and echo each tag to output. We use the PHP sort() function to sort the tags alphabetically, then the rsort() function to sort them in reverse.

PHP has a long list of functions for working with arrays. You can pull data from the middle of an array, pop it off the end, add more to the beginning, pretty much anything you can think to do. So once you have your tags in an array, you have a whole set of programming tools at your disposal.

Try It Out: Getting Related Tags

Every so often Flickr adds a new method to its API to increase the list of toys at your disposal. Sometimes they appear so quickly that there isn't a chance to add a wrapper to them to the Phlickr library. However, you can always use the Phlickr_Api class to call any of the Flickr API functions. This is the case with the related tags function of the Flickr API. Let's take a look at creating a custom API request and returning values from it.

```php
<?php
//tag_surf.php

$script_filename = basename($_REQUEST['SCRIPT_FILENAME']);
$searchtag = $_REQUEST["searchtag"];

?>

<html>
  <head>
    <title>Related Tags</title>
  </head>

  <body>

    <form method='get' action='<?php echo $script_filename; ?>'>
      <p>enter a tag <input type='text' name='searchtag' ➥
          value='<?php echo $searchtag; ?>' /></p>
      <input type='submit' value='search for related tags'/>
    </form>

    <?php
    if ($searchtag != '') {
      define('API_CONFIG_FILE', './authtoken.dat');

      require_once 'Phlickr/Api.php';

      // set up the api connection
      $api = Phlickr_Api::createFrom(API_CONFIG_FILE);

      if (! $api->isAuthValid()) {
        die("invalid flickr logon");
      }

      $request = $api->createRequest(
        'flickr.tags.getRelated',
        array('tag' => $searchtag)
      );
```

```php
    $response = $request->execute();
    $xml = $response->xml->tags;
?>


The tags related to <?php echo $searchtag; ?> are:<br/>

<?php
  $tag_counter = 0;
  foreach ($xml->tag as $tag) {
?>

<a href="<?php echo $script_filename; ?>?searchtag=<?php echo $tag; ?>">
  <?php echo $tag; ?></a>

  <?php
    flush();
    $tag_counter++;
  }

  if ($tag_counter == 0){
    print 'There are no related tags';
  }
}
?>

  </body>
</html>
```

When you open this example in a browser, you will get a text input box where you can enter a tag. When you submit the tag, you will get a list of hyperlinked, related tags. Click on any of the links, and you will get the tags related to that particular tag, as shown in Figure 7-2.

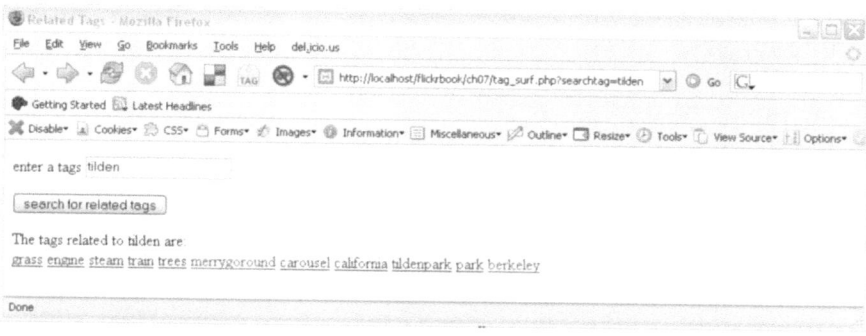

Figure 7-2. *Displaying related tags*

How It Works

In this example we create an HTML form that we can use to supply a tag to a custom API request using the `Phlickr_Api->createRequest()` method. This method requires two arguments. The first one is a string with the name of the Flickr API method. In this case, the method we are using is `flickr.tags.getRelated`. The second argument is a PHP array with the parameters for the Flickr method. Each Flickr method requires different parameters, so you will need to consult the Flickr API documentation to see exactly what you will need to supply.

In this case, since the `Phlickr_Api` object supplies the `api_key` parameter when we create the request, we need supply only one additional parameter: the `tag` parameter that indicates the tag that we want to find the related tags for. In this example, we've set the variable `$searchtag` to `tilden`.

```
$request = $api->createRequest(
 'flickr.tags.getRelated',
  array('tag' => $searchtag)
);
```

This code creates a `Phlickr_Request` object and stores it in the variable $request. The next step is to use the `execute()` method of the `Phlickr_Request` object, which returns a `Phlickr_Response` object, which returns an XML document from Flickr.

```
$response = $request->execute();
```

From there, we can retrieve the XML that we are interested in from the $response object. Again, the XML you receive as a response will depend on the Flickr API method that you are calling, so you will need to be familiar with the types of responses that each method returns.

To demonstrate, we'll take a look at the output from the $response object. In this case, the output of the `Phlickr_Response` looks like the following (we've edited out items 2–7 in the interest of space):

```
SimpleXMLElement Object
(
    [tags] => SimpleXMLElement Object
        (
            [tag] => Array
                (
                    [0] => grass
                    [1] => engine
                    ...
                    [8] => tildenpark
                    [9] => park
                    [10] => berkeley
                )
        )
)
```

You can see that the `Phlickr_Response` object contains a `SimpleXMLElement` property object, and inside that object there is another `SimpleXMLElement` object called tags. Inside of that element there is an array of tags related to `tilden`. This is the data we are interested in, but in order to get it, we will need to specify which SimpleXMLElement object we are interested in. The relevant section in our code looks like the following:

```
$xml = $response->xml->tags;
```

Here we are assigning only part of the response included in the [tags] section to the variable $xml. In other words, we've assigned the SimpleXMLElement object tags to the variable $xml. Now that we have the data we are interested in, we can iterate over the tags object and store each tag in the $tag variable.

```php
<?php
  $tag_counter = 0;
  foreach ($xml->tag as $tag) {
?>

<a href="<?php echo $script_filename; ?>?searchtag=<?php echo $tag; ?>">
  <?php echo $tag; ?></a>

  <?php
    flush();
    $tag_counter++;
  }
```

We then simply print the results to the browser.

Try It Out: Getting a User's Tags

We can also get the whole list of the tags that a particular user has tagged their photos with. Alternatively, we can get a short list of just the ones they use the most. To do this, we use the getUserTags() and the getPopularUserTags() methods, respectively, of the Phlickr_User object.

```php
<?php
//user_tags.php

define('API_CONFIG_FILE', './authtoken.dat');

require_once 'Phlickr/Api.php';
require_once 'Phlickr/User.php';

// set up the api connection

$api = Phlickr_Api::createFrom(API_CONFIG_FILE);

if (! $api->isAuthValid()) {
  die("invalid flickr logon");
}

$username = $_REQUEST['username'];
$script_filename = basename($_REQUEST['SCRIPT_FILENAME']);
?>
```

```
<html>
  <head>
    <title>Accessing Tags</title>
  </head>

  <body>

    <form method='post' action='<?php echo $script_filename; ?>'>
      <p>enter a flickr username: <input type='text' name='username' ➥
          value="<?php echo $username; ?>"/></p>
      <input type='submit' value='find tags for this user'/>
    </form>

    <?php
    if ($username != '') {
      $u = Phlickr_User::findByUsername($api, $username);

      $usertags = $u->getTags();
      $populartags = $u->getPopularTags('5');
    ?>

    All of this user's tags are:<br/>

    <?php
      foreach ($usertags as $tag) {
        print $tag.' ';
        flush();
      }
    ?>

    <br/><br/>
    The most popular tags are:<br/>

    <?php
      foreach ($populartags as $tag) {
        print $tag.' ';
        flush();
      }
    }
    ?>
  </body>
</html>
```

When you run this code in a browser, you will get a text input box where you can type in a user name. When you click the "find tags for this user" button, you will get two sets of tags: one with all the tags of the particular user you've specified, and a short list with only the most popular (most used) tags, as shown in Figure 7-3.

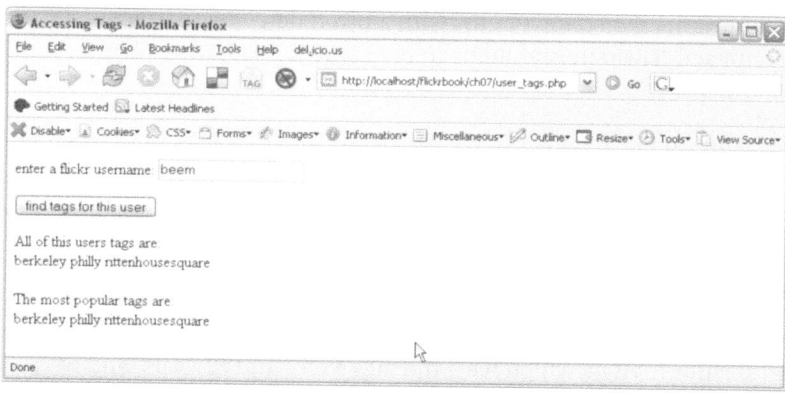

Figure 7-3. *Getting a user's tags*

How It Works

In this example we create a `Phlickr_User` object by specifying the user ID of the Flickr user we are interested in:

```
$u = Phlickr_User::findByUsername($api, $username);
```

We use the `getTags()` method and the `getPopularTags()` method of the `Phlickr_User` object to return all of the user's tags, then just the top five most popular tags:

```
$usertags = $u->getTags();
$populartags = $u->getPopularTags('5');
```

Notice that you can specify how many popular tags you want to return by changing the argument of the `getPopularTags()` method.

Try It Out: Searching by Tags

You can also call on the API to perform searches by tags. To do this, you will need to create a custom API request using the `Phlickr_Api` class. As you have seen in our previous example, when you create a custom API request, you can supply Flickr with various optional parameters. The `flickr.photos.search` method has a long list of optional parameters that you can use to define the photos you want to search for. We'll look at only a few important ones here. Keep in mind that all of these are optional. The only required parameter is the `api_key` parameter, which is supplied by Phlickr when you create the request.

- `user_id`: The ID of the user whose photo to search. If this parameter isn't passed, then everybody's public photos will be searched.

- `tags`: A comma-delimited list of tags. Photos with one or more of the tags listed will be returned.

- `tag_mode`: Either `any` for an OR combination of tags or `all` for an AND combination. Defaults to any.

- min_taken_date: Minimum taken date. Photos with a taken date greater than or equal to this value will be returned. The date should be in the MySQL DATETIME format, which is yyyy-mm-dd hh:MM:ss.

- max_taken_date: Maximum taken date. Photos with a taken date less than or equal to this value will be returned. The date should be in the MySQL DATETIME format.

- sort: The order in which to sort returned photos. The possible values are: date-posted-asc, date-posted-desc, date-taken-asc, date-taken-desc, interestingness-asc, interestingness-desc, and relevance. Defaults to date-posted-desc.

So to put these options into practice, we'll create a request to search only our own photos, taken between three and six months ago, which have the tags party and friends, and we will sort the results by their interestingness.

```php
<?php
//tag_request.php

define('API_CONFIG_FILE', './authtoken.dat');

require_once 'Phlickr/Api.php';
require_once 'Phlickr/PhotoList.php';
require_once 'Phlickr/PhotoListIterator.php';

// set up the api connection
$api = Phlickr_Api::createFrom(API_CONFIG_FILE);
if (! $api->isAuthValid()) {
  die("invalid flickr logon");
}

$tags = 'dance, performance';
$tagmode = 'all';
$userid =  $api->getUserId();
$sort = 'interestingness-desc';
$date3monthsago = date("Y-m-d G:i:s", strtotime("-3 months"));
$date6monthsago = date("Y-m-d G:i:s", strtotime("-6 months"));

$request = $api->createRequest(
  'flickr.photos.search',
```

```php
  array(
    'tags' => $tags,
    'tag_mode' => $tagmode,
    'user_id' => $userid,
    'min_taken_date' => $date6monthsago,
    'max_taken_date' => $date3monthsago,
    'sort' => $sort
  )
);

$pl = new Phlickr_PhotoList($request, Phlickr_PhotoList::PER_PAGE_MAX);
$pli = new Phlickr_PhotoListIterator($pl);
?>

<html>
  <head>
    <title>Searching Tags</title>
  </head>

  <body>
    <?php
    foreach ($pli->getPhotos() as $photo) {
    ?>

    title: <?php echo $photo->getTitle(); ?><br/>
    photo id: <a href="<?php echo $photo->buildUrl(); ?>">
      <?php echo $photo->getId(); ?></a><br/>

    <img src="<?php echo $photo->buildImgUrl('m'); ?>"/><br/><br/>

    <?php
    }
    ?>
  </body>
</html>
```

When the file is viewed in a browser, you will get a list of photos that meet the criteria you've specified, as well as the image and a link to the photo's page, as shown in Figure 7-4. The first photo listed is the photo that's deemed most interesting based on Flickr's interestingness algorithm.

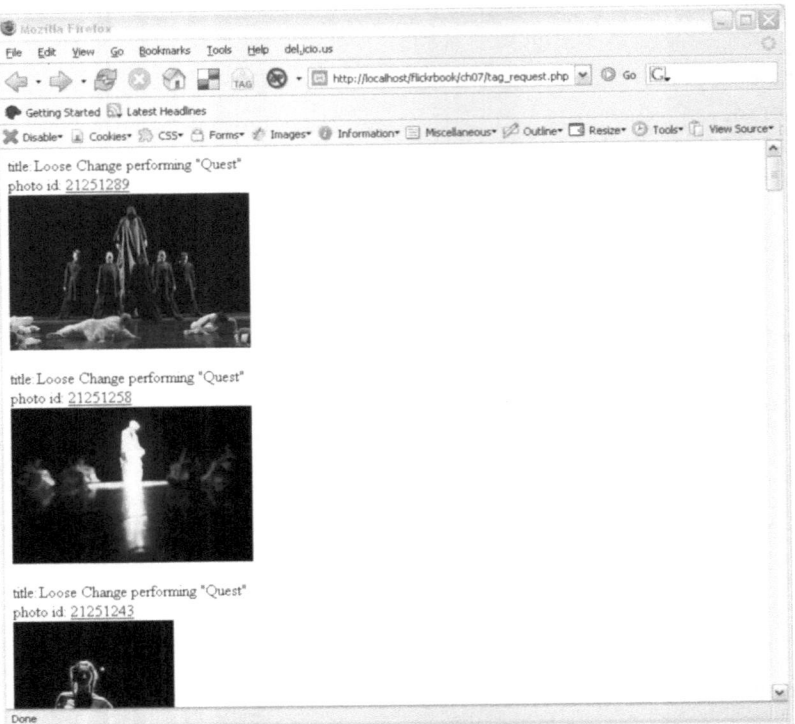

Figure 7-4. *The list of photos found with our search*

How It Works

In this example we've created a request to the flickr.photos.search method using the
Phlickr_Api class. To make the example clear, we've set up some variables that we will pass as
parameters.

```
$tags = 'dance, performance';
$tagmode = 'all';
$userid =  $api->getUserId();
$sort = 'interestingness-desc';
$date3monthsago = date("Y-m-d G:i:s", strtotime("-3 months"));
$date6monthsago = date("Y-m-d G:i:s", strtotime("-6 months"));
```

Notice that the $tags variable has a comma-separated list of tags. We could have chosen to use
only a single tag here, or we could have included up to 20 different tags. The $tagmode variable
is set to all, which means the photos must have both the tags dance and performance.

For the user ID, we've specified our own user ID by calling on the getUserId() method of
the Phlickr_Api class. The dates must be in the MySQL DATETIME format, so we used the
PHP date() function, which takes a Unix timestamp and formats it according to the format
supplied in the first argument. The PHP strtotime() function takes a human-readable string
value for its argument and returns a Unix timestamp. Once we have these variables in place,
we can create the Flickr API request using Phlickr's createRequest() method.

```php
$request = $api->createRequest(
  'flickr.photos.search',
  array(
    'tags' => $tags,
    'tag_mode' => $tagmode,
    'user_id' => $userid,
    'min_taken_date' => $date6monthsago,
    'max_taken_date' => $date3monthsago,
    'sort' => $sort
  )
);
```

From this request we create a `Phlickr_Photolist`, iterate through the photos, and return the ID and URL specific to the photo, as well as a small version of the image.

```php
$pl = new Phlickr_PhotoList($request, Phlickr_PhotoList::PER_PAGE_MAX);
$pli = new Phlickr_PhotoListIterator($pl);
?>

<html>
  <head>
    <title>Searching Tags</title>
  </head>

  <body>
    <?php
    foreach ($pli->getPhotos() as $photo) {
    ?>

    title: <?php echo $photo->getTitle(); ?><br/>
    photo id: <a href="<?php echo $photo->buildUrl(); ?>">
      <?php echo $photo->getId(); ?></a><br/>

    <img src="<?php echo $photo->buildImgUrl('m'); ?>"/><br/><br/>

    <?php
    }
    ?>
  </body>
</html>
```

Try It Out: Changing a Tag

At some point you've probably uploaded a batch of images with a certain tag but realized you should have used a different tag. The only way to fix it through the Flickr interface is to go through each photo individually, erase the tag, and type in the new one.

Now that you know how to find all of your photos with a particular tag and access the individual tags, changing a tag on all of your photos is a snap. You might remember from Chapter 5 that we used the Phlickr_AuthedPhoto object to write tags to a photo. We'll use that here again to fix a mistakenly applied tag.

I have a bad habit of spelling *performance* as *performace*. So for this example, we'll go through all my photos and do a tag search and replace.

```php
<?php
//tag_switch.php

define('API_CONFIG_FILE', './authtoken.dat');

require_once 'Phlickr/Api.php';
require_once 'Phlickr/PhotoList.php';
require_once 'Phlickr/PhotoListIterator.php';
require_once 'Phlickr/AuthedPhoto.php';

// set up the api connection
$api = Phlickr_Api::createFrom(API_CONFIG_FILE);
if (! $api->isAuthValid()) {
  die("invalid flickr logon");
}

$mistaketag = 'performace';
$newtag = 'performance';
$userid =  $api->getUserId();

$request = $api->createRequest(
  'flickr.photos.search',
  array(
    'tags' => $mistaketag,
    'user_id' => $userid
  )
);

$pl = new Phlickr_PhotoList($request, Phlickr_PhotoList::PER_PAGE_MAX);
$pli = new Phlickr_PhotoListIterator($pl);

foreach ($pli->getPhotos() as $photo) {
  $authedphoto = new Phlickr_AuthedPhoto($api, $photo->getId());
  $tagarray = $authedphoto->getTags();
  print_r($tagarray);
  $key = array_search($mistaketag, $tagarray);
  $tagarray[$key] = $newtag;
  $authedphoto->setTags($tagarray);
  print_r ($authedphoto->getTags());
  flush();
}
?>
```

When run, this code will produce two arrays for each instance it finds of the incorrect tag. The first one is the unedited version; the second is the new set of tags that have been written to the photo. Notice that my error has been fixed in the second tag array.

```
Array
(
    [0] => loosechange
    [1] => dance
    [2] => performace
    [3] => hiphop
    [4] => swing
)
Array
(
    [0] => loosechange
    [1] => dance
    [2] => performance
    [3] => hiphop
    [4] => swing
)
```

How It Works

The first step in this example is to find all of my photos with the mistaken tag. To do this, we create a Flickr API request to `flickr.photos.search`.

```
$mistaketag = 'performace';
$newtag = 'performance';
$userid = $api->getUserId();

$request = $api->createRequest(
  'flickr.photos.search',
  array(
    'tags' => $mistaketag,
    'user_id' => $userid
  )
);
```

Notice that we've left out the options such as `min_taken_date` and `sort`, which aren't important to us. The only thing we are concerned with here is finding all of the photos that have a misspelled tag.

We then make the request and iterate over the photos in the same fashion as in the last example. This time, however, we create a new `Phlickr_AuthedPhoto` object that corresponds to each photo we find.

```
foreach ($pli->getPhotos() as $photo) {
  $authedphoto = new Phlickr_AuthedPhoto($api, $photo->getId());
  $tagarray = $authedphoto->getTags();
  print_r($tagarray);
```

Since the tags of the `Phlickr_AuthedPhoto` object are writable, we can then make adjustments to the tags. To do this, we use the PHP `array_search()` function, which searches the values for a given string and returns the key of item. In this case, the string we are searching for is the misspelled tag, and it returns the value 2 to the variable $key.

```
$key = array_search($mistaketag, $tagarray);
```

Now that we know which item of the array is the offending tag, we can change it to the proper spelling.

```
$tagarray[$key] = $newtag;
```

We write the new, corrected tag array to the photo using the `setTags()` method and show the results using `print_r()`.

```
$authedphoto->setTags($tagarray);
print_r ($authedphoto->getTags());
```

Assigning Tags While Uploading

Everyone who takes a lot of photos has their own system of managing their images. For instance, maybe you dump all the photos taken on a particular day into a directory on your computer, or maybe you change the file name on the images to describe what is in the photo. Perhaps you don't use a digital camera that automatically assigns a date taken to your photos; instead you scan film negatives and store them on your computer.

While the Flickr Uploadr makes uploading a batch of images and assigning a set of tags to all the photos in the batch quite easy, it might not be exactly the right tool to use for someone who has a more complex imaging work flow. This is especially true if you shoot film and then upload the scanned images. Since the scanned images aren't stamped with the date they are taken, you would then have to go back and change the date on each photo you've uploaded.

The following example shows how you could use Phlickr to customize a work flow. Say for instance, you shoot film, then save the scanned images to a directory that you label with the date they were taken. For instance, you might put all the images in a directory named 10_aug_2004. You then rename all of the images to describe the people and events in the photos. So you might have photos called Andrew_happyhour.jpg or winter_snow_driving.jpg. You'd like to be able to just upload the images and have the titles of the photos set to the file name; for instance, "andrew happyhour" would be the title of the first file. You'd also like the words to become tags for your photos, as well as to be able to assign tags to the whole batch. Finally, you'd want to have the date taken set to August 10, 2004 for all of the photos.

Try It Out: Uploading and Tagging Photos

Using the Phlickr library, uploading and tagging photos is completely customizable. The following example is a utility program designed to run from the command line. If you've included the php executable in your PATH variable, you only need to type php. In our case this looks like:

```
$ php uploader.php
```

Let's take a look at the code.

```php
<?php
//uploader.php

define('API_CONFIG_FILE', './authtoken.dat');
define('UPLOAD_DIRECTORY', 'C:\\photos\\10_aug_2004');
define('PHOTO_EXTENSION', '.jpg');

require_once 'Phlickr/Api.php';
require_once 'Phlickr/Uploader.php';
require_once 'Phlickr/AuthedPhoto.php';

$api = Phlickr_Api::createFrom(API_CONFIG_FILE);
if (! $api->isAuthValid()) {
  die("invalid flickr logon");
}

$uploader = new Phlickr_Uploader($api);
$di = new DirectoryIterator(UPLOAD_DIRECTORY);

$additionaltags = getAdditionalTags();
$datetaken = directoryForDates();

foreach($di as $item) {
  // only files with the given extension...

  if ($item->isFile()) {
    if (substr(strtolower($item), - strlen(PHOTO_EXTENSION)) ➥
        === strtolower(PHOTO_EXTENSION)) {
      print "Uploading $item...\r\n";

      $title = str_replace('_', ' ', rtrim(strtolower($item), '.jpg'));
      $phototags = $additionaltags.' '.$title;
      $new_photo_id = ➥
        $uploader->upload($item->getPathname(), $title, '', $phototags);
```

```php
      if ($datetaken){
        $ap = new Phlickr_AuthedPhoto($api, $new_photo_id);
        $ap->setTaken($datetaken);
      }

      $photo_ids[] = $new_photo_id;
    }
  }
}

if (count($photo_ids)) {
  printf("\r\nAll done! If you care to make some changes:\r\n%s", ➥
          $uploader->buildEditUrl($photo_ids));
}

function getAdditionalTags() {

  print 'List of additional tags, separated by spaces, if any: ';
  // trim any whitespace
  $tags = trim(fgets(STDIN));

  if ($tags) {
    print "The photos will be tagged with '" . $tags . "'.\r\n\r\n";
  } else {
    print "The photos will not have any additional tags.\r\n\r\n";
  }
  return $tags;
}

function directoryForDates() {

  $dirbasename = basename(UPLOAD_DIRECTORY);

  print "Use directory info as date taken? Currently:$dirbasename (y/N): ";

  $datetaken = date("Y-m-d G:i:s", strtotime(str_replace('_', ' ', $dirbasename)));

  $reply = trim(fgets(STDIN));

  if ($reply == 'y') {
    print "Date taken will be set to '" . $datetaken. "'.\r\n\r\n";
    return $datetaken;
  } else {
    print "Photos will set to current time tagged with the current time.\r\n\r\n";
  }
}

?>
```

When you run this code from the command line, you will get output similar to the following:

```
List of additional tags, separated by spaces, if any: blackandwhite film 35mm
The photos will be tagged with 'blackandwhite film 35mm'.

Use directory info as date taken? Currently:10_aug_2004 (y/N): y
Date taken will be set to '2004-08-10 0:00:00'.

Uploading andrew_happyhour.JPG...
Uploading snow_eastcoast_trees_february.JPG...
Uploading writersanonymous_coffee.JPG...

All done! If you care to make some changes:
http://www.flickr.com/tools/uploader_edit.gne?ids=95703452,95703483,95703496
```

How It Works

In addition to the classes we've used in previous examples, this time we use the `Phlickr_Uploader` class. As its name implies, this class handles uploading of files. Simply pass it a full path and file name, a title, a description, and a set of tags, and it will manage uploading the file to your Flickr account.

So to start with, we create a new `Phlickr_Uploader` object and save it in the variable `$uploader`.

```
$uploader = new Phlickr_Uploader($api);
```

We create a PHP directory iterator object and point it to the directory where we've saved our files:

```
$di = new DirectoryIterator(UPLOAD_DIRECTORY);
```

We use two custom functions to get information from the user. The first function, `getAdditionalTags()`, asks the user if they want to supply additional tags other than just the tags stored in the file name itself.

```
function getAdditionalTags() {

  print 'List of additional tags, separated by spaces, if any: ';
  // trim any whitespace
  $tags = trim(fgets(STDIN));

  if ($tags) {
    print "The photos will be tagged with '" . $tags . "'.\r\n\r\n";
  } else {
    print "The photos will not have any additional tags.\r\n\r\n";
  }
  return $tags;
}
```

In this case we chose the additional tags blackandwhite, film, and 35mm. We read in the information from the command line using the PHP fgets(STDIN) function. getAdditionalTags()returns the list of tags back to the the $additionaltags variable, unless the user leaves this blank.

```
$additionaltags = getAdditionalTags();
```

We then call the directoryForDates() function, which gets the folder that the photos are stored in and asks the user if they want to use the folder as a source for the date to stamp the date taken property of the uploaded photos. This function uses the date(), strtotime(), and str_replace() functions to put the folder name into MySQL DATETIME format:

```
function directoryForDates() {

  $dirbasename = basename(UPLOAD_DIRECTORY);

  print "Use directory info as date taken? Currently: $dirbasename (y/N): ";

  $datetaken = date("Y-m-d G:i:s", strtotime(str_replace('_', ' ', $dirbasename)));

  $reply = trim(fgets(STDIN));

  if ($reply == 'y') {
    print "Date taken will be set to '" . $datetaken. "'.\r\n\r\n";
    return $datetaken;
  } else {
    print "Photos will set to current time tagged with the current time.\r\n\r\n";
  }
}
```

If the user answers y, the results of this function are returned into the $datetaken variable. Otherwise the user is informed that the current time will be used.

```
$datetaken = directoryForDates();
```

Once we've collected the information we need from the user, we iterate over the contents of the directory, looking only for files with the .jpg extension. To accomplish this, we use a simple string comparison.

```
if (substr(strtolower($item), - strlen(PHOTO_EXTENSION)) ➡
    === strtolower(PHOTO_EXTENSION)) {
```

If this checks out, we begin preparing the file for upload. First we create a title for the photo by removing the underscores and file extension from the photo.

```
$title = str_replace('_', ' ', rtrim(strtolower($item), '.jpg'));
```

We create a set of tags for the photo, combining the title string with the additional tags that we've specified earlier.

```
$phototags = $additionaltags.' '.$title;
```

We upload the file. We also store the resulting photo ID in a variable called $new_photo_id.

```
$new_photo_id = $uploader->upload($item->getPathname(), $title, '', $phototags);
```

We check to see if the user has decided to use the folder name for the date taken. If they have, we create a new Phlickr_AuthedPhoto object and set it to the image we've just uploaded, using our newly created photo ID.

```
$ap = new Phlickr_AuthedPhoto($api, $new_photo_id);
```

We set the date taken property of the photo using the setTaken() method.

```
$ap->setTaken($datetaken);
```

Once our photo is set to the date we want, we store the photo ID in an array with the photo IDs of any other images we've uploaded.

```
$photo_ids[] = $new_photo_id;
```

Finally, when we've uploaded all the photos, we create a URL that directs the user to the files that have just been uploaded in case they want to make any further changes.

```
printf("\r\nAll done! If you care to make some changes:\r\n%s", ➥
        $uploader->buildEditUrl($photo_ids));
```

That's it; we've just made our own custom uploader to handle what would be an otherwise time-consuming task.

Summary

In this chapter we looked at several ways that you can put Flickr tags to use. We've covered accessing the tags, changing them, searching by tags, and uploading files with custom tags. The intention of this chapter is to show you the basics, but hopefully trying out these examples will inspire some novel uses. You could, for instance, create a PHP program that parses recent news stories for keywords, then pulls Flickr photos with matching tags: a sort of illustrated news blog. Or perhaps you could make a site that matches users who have similar interests based on similar tags. Possibly you would want to make an automatic blog that constantly searches the latest photos posted to Flickr with certain tags. Maybe you might want to create a tag translator that automatically adds tags in a different language. The Flickr API makes all these ideas possible.

In the next chapter, we'll look at accessing the various RSS feeds that Flickr produces and find out how you can use them in your own website.

CHAPTER 8

■ ■ ■

RSS Feeds and Syndication

For some tasks, like tracking photos added to a group pool or recent activity on your account, there's an easy alternative to Flickr's API. Using PHP 5's new SimpleXML extension, you can easily parse Flickr's RSS feeds. For other tasks, like viewing a photo's or group's comments, the RSS feed is the only way to access the information.

In Chapter 2 we discussed the basic ways that you could view Flickr's RSS feeds using an aggregator. In this chapter we will expand on that by

- Discussing in more depth RSS and the feeds that Flickr provides

- Looking at the basics of the XML format

- Using the SimpleXML extension to parse RSS feeds

What Is RSS?

RSS is a lightweight XML schema to allow websites to present structured data about content they've posted. The structure lets visitors and other websites use the data for a multitude of different purposes. RSS is used for an ever-increasing list of tasks, including publishing lists of recent news stories or blog posts via email or podcasts.

The only downside of RSS, and it's really a minor one, is the number of incompatible formats that are lumped together under the title RSS. You've probably heard that old saw, "The nice thing about standards is there are so many to choose from." Well, it is never truer than when talking about RSS.

The original RSS, version 0.9, was developed by Netscape in 1999 to exchange headlines between their sites. Netscape lost interest in further development of the format, but another company, UserLand Software, continued to develop the standard. In the meantime, a group of noncommercial interests began work on a version of the standard that more closely followed the ideas set out in the original 0.9, releasing 0.91 and eventually 1.0. UserLand wasn't happy with the other group's work and continued development, releasing several incompatible versions: 0.91, 0.92, 0.93, and then, to the annoyance of the other group, 2.0.

The Atom format was created in an attempt to address some of the perceived shortcomings of the RSS 2.0 format. The RSS 2.0 specification is copyrighted by Harvard University. The specification dictates that if any significant changes are made to the format, it must be done under a different name, hence, Atom. Atom 0.3 was released in December 2003 and, even in its early draft state, was widely adopted. The final draft of the Atom 1.0 specification was published in July 2005. In December 2005, Atom 1.0 began the process of becoming an official standard of the Internet Engineering Task Force. Currently, most software, including Flickr, is still using Atom 0.3, but it would be reasonable to assume that once the format is standardized, its use will become much more widespread.

To give you an idea of the differences in the structure, we'll compare examples of the three most widely supported formats—RSS 1.0, RSS 2.0, and Atom 0.3—and then we'll look briefly at the new Atom 1.0.

RSS 1.0

Here is an example of an RSS 1.0 document. It is based on the Resource Description Framework (RDF), which provides a way to describe resources on the Internet. For more information on the RSS 1.0 specification, visit http://web.resource.org/rss/1.0/.

```
<?xml version="1.0"?>
<rdf:RDF
  xmlns:rdf="http://www.w3.org/1999/02/22-rdf-syntax-ns#"
  xmlns="http://purl.org/rss/1.0/"
>
  <channel rdf:about="http://www.example.com/xml/news.rss">
    <title>Example Feed</title>
    <link>http://example.com/</link>
    <description>Description of the feed</description>
    <image rdf:resource="http://example.com/images/xml_tiny.gif" />
    <items>
      <rdf:Seq>
        <rdf:li resource="http://example.com/pub/rss1" />
      </rdf:Seq>
    </items>
  </channel>

  <item rdf:about="http://example.com/pub/rss1">
    <title>RSS Powered Robots Run Amok</title>
    <link>http://example.com/pub/rss1</link>
    <description>Some text.</description>
  </item>
</rdf:RDF>
```

RSS 2.0

RSS 2.0 doesn't use RDF semantics; it defines its own tags. For more information on the RSS 2.0 specification, visit http://blogs.law.harvard.edu/tech/rss/.

```
<?xml version="1.0"?>
<rss version="2.0">
  <channel>
    <title>Example Feed</title>
    <link>http://example.com/</link>
```

```
    <description>Description of the feed.</description>
    <language>en-us</language>
    <pubDate>Tue, 10 Jun 2003 04:00:00 GMT</pubDate>

    <lastBuildDate>Tue, 10 Jun 2003 09:41:01 GMT</lastBuildDate>
    <docs>http://blogs.law.harvard.edu/tech/rss</docs>
    <generator>Example Generator 2.0</generator>
    <managingEditor>editor@example.com</managingEditor>
    <webMaster>webmaster@example.com</webMaster>
    <item>
      <title>RSS Powered Robots Run Amok</title>
      <link>http://example.com/pub/rss2</link>
      <description>Some text.</description>
      <pubDate>Tue, 03 Jun 2003 09:39:21 GMT</pubDate>
      <guid>http://example.com/pub/rss1</guid>
    </item>
  </channel>
</rss>
```

Atom 0.3

Neither Atom format uses RDF. Here's an example of an Atom 0.3 document. For more information on the Atom 0.3 specification, visit http://www.mnot.net/drafts/ draft-nottingham-atom-format-02.html.

```
<?xml version="1.0" encoding="utf-8"?>
<feed version="0.3" xmlns="http://purl.org/atom/ns#">
  <title>Example Feed</title>
  <link rel="alternate" type="text/html" href="http://example.com/"/>
  <modified>2003-12-13T18:30:02Z</modified>
  <author>
    <name>John Doe</name>
  </author>

  <entry>
    <title>Atom-Powered Robots Run Amok</title>
    <link rel="alternate" type="text/html" href="http://example.com/pub/atom"/>
    <id>tag:example.com,2003:12345</id>
    <modified>2003-12-13T18:30:02Z</modified>
    <issued>2003-12-13T18:30:02Z</issued>
    <summary>Some text.</summary>
  </entry>
</feed>
```

Atom 1.0

Here's an example of an Atom 1.0 document. For more information on the Atom 1.0 specification, visit http://www.ietf.org/rfc/rfc4287.txt.

```
<?xml version="1.0" encoding="utf-8"?>
<feed xmlns="http://www.w3.org/2005/Atom">
  <title>Example Feed</title>
  <link href="http://example.com/"/>
  <updated>2003-12-13T18:30:02Z</updated>
  <author>
    <name>John Doe</name>
  </author>
  <id>urn:uuid:60a76c80-d399-11d9-b93C-0003939e0af6</id>

  <entry>
    <title>Atom-Powered Robots Run Amok</title>
    <link href="http://example.com/pub/atom"/>
    <id>tag:example.com,2003:12345</id>
    <updated>2003-12-13T18:30:02Z</updated>
    <summary>Some text.</summary>
  </entry>
</feed>
```

Choosing a Format

With all the different syndication formats you may be asking yourself, which should I choose? Fortunately, Flickr supports a majority of the most popular syndication formats (RSS 0.91, 0.92, 1.0, 2.0, and Atom 0.3), so all you need to do is pick one. By default, Flickr returns Atom 0.3 feeds. You can read more about the various feed formats that Flickr supports at http://flickr.com/services/feeds/.

What Information Does Flickr Provide as RSS Feeds?

Flickr provides feeds for a large portion of the site's data. This section lists the URLs in their most basic forms.

Public Photos by User or Tag

This URL lets you search for the latest public photos by user or tag: http://flickr.com/services/feeds/photos_public.gne. There are several optional parameters you can provide to limit the photos listed in the feed. If no parameters are provided, the results will be from the most recently added public photos.

- `id`: Specifies a user ID to limit the photos to a single user

- `ids`: Provides a comma-separated list of user IDs to limit the photos to a group of users

- `tags`: Provides a comma-separated list of tags limit the photos to those containing any of the tags

Contact's Photos

This method lets you view photos uploaded by a user's contacts. The user can be you, a friend, or anyone else on the site. Replace USERID with the user ID of an existing Flickr user: `http://flickr.com/services/feeds/photos_friends.gne?user_id=USERID@N0O`.

There are two optional parameters to modify the photos listed in the feed.

- `friends`: Omitting this parameter or setting it to 0 will return photos uploaded by any of the user's contacts. Setting this parameter to 1 will limit the list to only photos uploaded by friends and family.

- `display_all`: Omitting this parameter or setting it to 0 will limit the results to a single photo per contact. Setting this to 1 will display several of the user's contacts' photos.

Comments About a User's Photos

This URL lists all the recent activity on a user's photos. Replace USERID with the ID of an existing Flickr user: `http://flickr.com/recent_comments_feed.gne?id=USERID@N0O`.

Comments Made by a User

This URL provides a list of all the recent comments that a user has made to their and others' photos. Replace USERID with the ID of an existing Flickr user: `http://flickr.com/photos_comments_feed.gne?user_id=USERID@N0O`.

Group Photo Pool

This URL lists recent photos posted to a Flickr group pool. Replace GROUPID with the ID of an existing Flickr group: `http://flickr.com/groups/GROUPID@N0O/pool/feed/`.

Group Comments

This URL lists recent comments posted to a group's discussion. Replace GROUPID with the ID of an existing Flickr group: `http://flickr.com/groups_feed.gne?id=GROUPID@N0O`.

Feed Formats

You can request that the feed be returned in a specific feed format by appending a `format` parameter to any of the URLs. For example, to retrieve recent, public photos as an Atom feed, you would use the following URL:

`http://www.flickr.com/services/feeds/photos_public.gne?`**`format=atom`**

For a complete list of the supported feed formats, see Table 8-1.

Table 8-1. *Supported Flickr Syndication Formats*

Parameter Value	Format Description
atom, atom_03	An Atom 0.3 formatted feed
rss_091	An RSS 0.91 formatted feed
rss_092 or rss	An RSS 0.92 formatted feed
rss_100 or rdf	An RSS 1.0 formatted feed
rss_200	An RSS 2.0 formatted feed
rss_200_enc	An RSS 2.0 formatted feed with enclosures (but without enclosure sizes)

Tip Flickr provides a number of undocumented feed formats: csv (comma-separated values), json (JavaScript Object Notation), php (executable PHP code), php_serial (serialized PHP values), sql (Structured Query Language), and yaml (YAML Ain't Markup Language). These formats are undocumented and unsupported, but depending on what you're doing, they may be able to save you quite a bit of time converting formats.

Try It Out: Emailing Account Activity Updates

This recipe demonstrates how you can easily extract data from an Atom 0.3 RSS feed and reformat it for use in another medium. In this case, we'll use a recent activity feed and send an email with any updates. The RSS feed is in XML, so we'll make use of the XML knowledge we learned in the previous chapter.

```php
<?php
// flickr user id
define('USER_ID', '26159919@N00');
// email address where updates will be sent to
define('EMAIL', 'user@example.com');
// your mail host
define('SMTP_MAIL_HOST', 'mail.example.com');
// file where we track the last comment seen
define('CONFIG_FILE', '.lastFlickrComment');

// load id of the last entry we've seen from the file
if (file_exists(CONFIG_FILE)) {
  $lastSeen = file_get_contents(CONFIG_FILE);
} else {
  $lastSeen = '';
}
```

```php
// construct a url to the user's feed
$url = rawurlencode(
  'http://www.flickr.com/recent_comments_feed.gne?format=atom_03&id='. USER_ID
);
$xml = simplexml_load_file($url);

// loop through all the entries and build an email body
$body = '';
foreach ($xml->entry as $entry) {
  // make sure we haven't seen this entry before
  if ($lastSeen == (string) $entry->id) {
    break;
  }

  // first step, strip out the HTML formatting, the comments are
  // now in the format "UserX has posted a comment:\n\nCommentBody\n\n"
  $post = strip_tags($entry->content);
  // drop everything up to the colon
  $post = strstr($post, ":\n\n");
  // now, the drop the colon and two new lines we just matched
  $post = substr($post, 3);
  // remove any trailing characters
  $post = trim($post);
  // wrap any long lines
  $post = wordwrap($post);

  // put it all together
  $body .= "{$entry->title}:\n\"{$post}\" - {$entry->author->name}\n\n";
}

// if we've got any output, mail it off
if ($body) {
  // add a link to flickr's site, for good luck
  $body .= "See more: http://flickr.com/recent_activity.gne";

  // set up the mailing configuration ...
  ini_set('sendmail_from', EMAIL);
  ini_set('SMTP', SMTP_MAIL_HOST);
  // ... and send the mail
  $wasSent = mail(EMAIL, 'Flickr Updates', $body);

  // if the email sent, save the id of the newest entry so we know to skip
  // everything after it.
  if ($wasSent) {
    file_put_contents(CONFIG_FILE, (string) $xml->entry[0]->id);
  }
}
```

```
// you may want to uncomment the next line for testing
#print $body;
?>
```

Before running this script, you'll need to modify the constants at the top. If you're unsure of the SMTP_MAIL_HOST, check your ISP's website; they may refer to it as an SMTP server or outgoing mail server.

The first time you run this, you'll get an email that's something like the following:

```
To: user@example.com
From: user@example.com
Subject: Flickr Updates

Comment about paste up:
"i was once arrested for street art like this" - _sloppy_

Comment about warning:
"i tagged that bridge in 2000" - _sloppy_

Comment about Ascent Sculpture:
"love the clouds reflected on this

great perspective!" - carolyn_in_oregon

Comment about kung fu dream:
"nice!" - Precious Roy

Comment about billy nickey:
"god, i smoke too much" - Totally Robot

Comment about jockey club:
"Yes, but me first." - Dennis Dixson

See more: http://flickr.com/recent_activity.gne
```

If you run it again, unless someone has just posted a comment to your account, you won't get another email. If you delete the file named in CONFIG_FILE and rerun the script, another email will be sent.

How It Works

This is a pretty simple program. The idea is to grab the feed, loop through the entries, reformat them for email, and then send it off. The trick is that the next time it's run we don't want to email the same comments, and if there aren't any new comments, we don't want to send an email. We assume that Flickr presents all the comments in reverse chronological order, with the newest comments first and oldest last, so once we encounter a comment that we've already seen on a previous run, we can stop looking.

The first few lines of the script define the constants used in the script. As was already mentioned, before running the script you'll want to adjust these values. USER_ID should be set to the user ID of the Flickr account you'd like to monitor. EMAIL is the email address the list of comments will be sent to. SMTP_MAIL_HOST should be set to the name or IP address of your ISP's outgoing SMTP mail server. CONFIG_FILE is the file name of a file used to store the Atom ID of the last comment emailed to the user.

The first thing the script does is check whether the file named by the CONFIG_FILE constant exists. If it does, we load the contents using file_get_contents(). Next, we build a URL for the feed and use simplexml_load_file() to both retrieve the feed and parse it into a SimpleXML object.

The next block of code is where the real work of pulling the data from our feed and formatting it for the email happens. We use foreach to loop through all the entry elements in the feed. The first step is to check whether the entry's ID matches the one we loaded from the configuration file. If it does, we use the break to leave the loop. If it doesn't we start by using strip_tags() to remove all the HTML formatting from the comment. The next couple of steps remove some unneeded parts of the comment, and then we call wordwrap() to ensure that the output won't have any long, unwrapped lines that might be hard to read in an email client. Finally, we concatenate the entry's title, cleaned-up comment, and author name and add them to the body of our email.

Next, we check whether there's a body for our email. If there haven't been any new comments since the last time the script was run, $body will be the empty string (which is equivalent to FALSE). If we have a body, we use ini_set() to configure PHP's mail settings and call mail() to send the message.

The last step is to check whether the email was sent successfully. If the message wasn't sent, it doesn't make any sense to keep track of the last comment they've seen, because they'll never see it. If the email was sent properly, we can save the ID of the newest entry. Again, we're assuming that comments are in reverse chronological order. We'll write this value to the file defined in CONFIG_FILE using the file_put_contents() function. This value will be loaded the next time the script is run, so we can skip over any previously mailed comments.

Running the Script Automatically

For this script to really be useful, it needs to be run regularly. Fortunately, it's relatively easy to have the computer take care of this for you.

Under Windows XP

To automatically run programs on Windows you use the Scheduled Tasks function. To schedule a task under Windows, follow these steps:

1. Start ➤ Settings ➤ Control Panel ➤ Scheduled Tasks.

2. Double-click the Add Scheduled Task item.

3. After reading the introduction, click Next.

4. Click Browse, locate and select the PHP executable (php.exe), and click OK.

5. Choose what directory you'd like the script to be run in, and click Next.

6. Set the scheduling options, and click Next.

7. If you want the script to run when you're not logged on, enter a username and password.

8. Click Next.

9. Select the box next to "Open advanced properties for this task when I click Finish." Click Finish, and the advanced properties setting should appear. (You can also access the advanced properties by double-clicking the task's icon in the Scheduled Tasks folder.)

10. In the Run field, you'll need to add the full path to the script to the end of PHP's path, for example, `"C:\php\php.exe" "C:\example_dir\script_file.php"`. Obviously, you'll need to adjust the script's file name to point to the file on your computer. Make sure that both PHP and the script's file names are in double quotes.

11. Click OK.

12. In the Scheduled Tasks window, right-click on the newly created task and select Run from the pop-up menu. A command prompt window will briefly appear with the results of the script.

Scheduling Under Unix and OS X

Task scheduling under most Unix variants is done by a continuously running background program named `cron`. Once a minute, `cron` checks to see whether there are scheduled tasks to be run and, if so, it executes them. These tasks are called `cron` jobs. To schedule a `cron` job, you use the following command:

```
$ crontab -e
```

Your default editor will open with the contents of your user's crontab file. If you want to run a PHP script named `/home/user/script_file.php` every day at midnight, add the following line to the file:

```
0  0  *  *  *   /usr/local/bin/php /home/user/script.php
```

The `crontab` file uses a specific format to indicate which program should be run at which times. Each job is on its own line, and white space—spaces and tabs—are used to separate the fields. The order of the fields, from left to right, and their allowed ranges are as follows:

1. Minute (0–59)

2. Hour (0–23)

3. Day of month (1–31)

4. Month (1–12)

5. Day of week (0–6 where Sunday = 0)

6. Command to be run

The asterisk character is used to indicate that any value is acceptable. The hour, minute, and month fields operate as an AND operation. The following task would be run every time the minute is 15 and the hour is 6 (6:15 a.m.) each day:

```
15  6  *  *  *   /usr/local/bin/php /home/user/script.php
```

Counterintuitively, the day of month and day of week (the third and fifth) fields operate as an OR operation; when either one is true, the task will be run. For example, the following would be run at midnight every Monday and the first day of each month:

```
 0  0  1  *  1   /usr/local/bin/php /home/user/script.php
```

You can also specify multiple values for a single field by using commas to separate them. The following would run the task at midnight, 6 a.m., noon, and 6 p.m. every day:

```
 0  0,6,12,18  *  *  *    /usr/local/bin/php /home/user/script.php
```

We'll finish with a more complex example that runs every 20 minutes from 8 a.m. to 5 p.m. on weekdays:

```
0,20,40  8-17  *  *  1-5   /usr/local/bin/php /home/user/script.php
```

Using these samples, you should be able to schedule tasks.

Summary

In this chapter we've looked at the various RSS formats and a brief history of their development, as well as the way Flickr makes data available as feeds. Finally, we put it all together and built a script to convert a comment feed into a daily email. This included instructions on how to run the script automatically.

In the next chapter, we'll look at Flickr's groups and bring all our knowledge about Flickr and Phlickr together.

CHAPTER 9

Bringing Photos Together: Adding Collaborative Features to Your Website with Flickr Groups

Flickr groups are a great way for multiple photographers to unite and create a pool of related images. The list of groups seems endless, and if you've been a Flickr user for any length of time, you've probably been invited to join at least a few.

While Flickr provides a great interface for uploading and editing the metadata for photos in the group, the presentation of the group images is a little lacking in features. For instance, there is no way to sort the group by date, or look at the tags just for the group. Also you might want to have your photos displayed in a special layout.

In this chapter we will resolve these problems and demonstrate how to make a collaborative photo gallery site. As an example, we will be building a site for a kung fu school. We want to be able to have web galleries that show photos of each member of the group individually. We'll also have pages that display specific kung fu moves and events for the group. Finally, we'd like to display the latest posts to the group. This project will pull together some of the techniques we've used in previous chapters and explore using Flickr as the back end for a collaborative website.

Creating a Group

The first thing you will need to do is to create a new group. You're probably already familiar with creating groups, but if not, we covered this in Chapter 2, in the "Categorizing Photos" section. For our example, we've created a group called "East West Wing Chun Kung Fu Association," and the URL of the group is http://www.flickr.com/groups/eastwest/.

We've made the group "invite only," so only members of the group can add photos.

Batch Adding Photos to a Group

Next you'll need to have some photos in the group. Once you upload photos to Flickr, you have two choices for adding the photos to a group through the Flickr interface. You can look at each photo page individually, then click on the SEND TO GROUP icon above the photo and select the group from the list. Or, you can use Organizr and individually select the photos that you want to add to the group. Each of these methods requires you to add photos to a group one at a time and can be tedious if you have a lot of photos to add to a group.

Try It Out: Adding a Batch of Photos to a Group

Fortunately, you can easily use the API to add a batch of photos to a group. In the following example, we will take all of the photos with a specific tag (or tags) and add them to a group. You will need to be an administrator of the group in order to use this example.

```php
<?php
//batch_add_to_group.php

define('API_CONFIG_FILE', './authtoken.dat');

require_once 'Phlickr/Api.php';
require_once 'Phlickr/PhotoList.php';
require_once 'Phlickr/PhotoListIterator.php';
include_once 'Phlickr/AuthedGroup.php';

// set up the api connection
$api = Phlickr_Api::createFrom(API_CONFIG_FILE);
if (! $api->isAuthValid()) {
  die("invalid flickr logon");
}

$script_filename = basename($_REQUEST['SCRIPT_FILENAME']);
$tags = $_REQUEST["tags"];
$group_id = $_REQUEST["groupid"];
?>

<html>
  <head>
    <title>Add Tagged Photos to A Group</title>
  </head>

  <body>
    <form method='get' action='<?php echo $script_filename; ?>'>
      <p>
        enter a comma-separated list of tags
        <input type='text' name='tags' value='<?php echo $tags; ?>' />
        and enter the group id
        <input type='text' name='groupid' value='<?php echo $group_id; ?>' />
      </p>

      <input type='submit' value='add photos to the group'/>
    </form>
```

```php
<?php
if ($tags == '' or $group_id == '') {
  die('Please enter a tag or set of tags and a group id');
}

$request = $api->createRequest(
  'flickr.photos.search',
  array(
    'tags' => $tags,
    'tag_mode' => 'all',
    'user_id' => $api->getUserId()
    )
);

try {
  $pl = new Phlickr_PhotoList($request, Phlickr_PhotoList::PER_PAGE_MAX);
  $pli = new Phlickr_PhotoListIterator($pl);
  $ag = new Phlickr_AuthedGroup($api, $group_id);
} catch (Exception $e) {
  die ('Error: '. $e->getMessage(). "<br />");
}

foreach ($pli->getPhotos() as $photo) {
  $photoid = $photo->getId();
  try {
    $ag->add($photoid);
    echo 'adding photo '. $photoid, "<br />";
    flush();
  } catch (Exception $e) {
    echo 'Error: ', $e->getMessage(), "<br />";
    flush();
  }
}
?>
</body>
</html>
```

When you view this code in a web browser, you will see an HTML form that allows you to enter a comma-separated list of tags and a group ID. When you click the "add photos to the group" button, the images will be added to the group as shown in Figure 9-1.

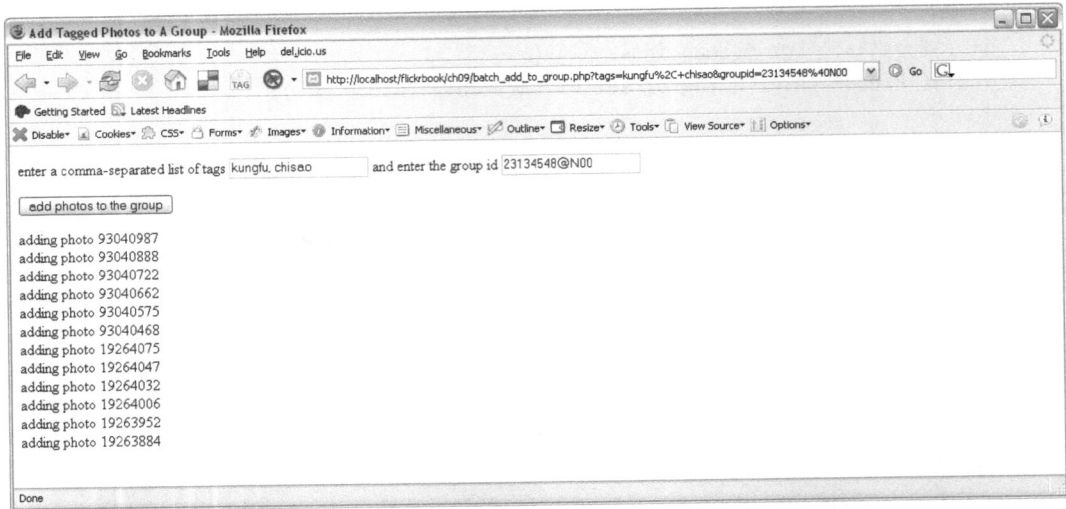

Figure 9-1. *Batch adding photos to a group*

If you run this script more than once using the same tags and group, you will get a message "photo already in pool," because each photo can be added only once to a group.

How It Works

This example works by creating a request using the Phlickr_API object. Here we are connecting to flickr.photos.search and selecting all of the photos that have the tags we've specified in your user account.

```
$request = $api->createRequest(
    'flickr.photos.search',
    array(
        'tags' => $tags,
        'tag_mode' => 'all',
        'user_id' => $api->getUserId()
    );
```

In our example we used only one tag to search on (kungfu), but we could have used several tags separated by commas and selected only photos that have both tags, since in this case the tag_mode is set to all.

Once we have stored the results of the API request in the $request variable, we create a Phlickr_PhotoList object from the results.

```
$pl = new Phlickr_PhotoList($request, Phlickr_PhotoList::PER_PAGE_MAX);
```

From there, we use the Phlickr_PhotoListIterator class, which iterates through the results and returns a list of photos.

```
$pli = new Phlickr_PhotoListIterator($pl);
```

We create a `Phlickr_AuthedGroup` object and set it to the group we want to add the photos to. In this case, we've supplied the `Phlickr_AuthedGroup` class with the ID of the group (78064184@N00).

```
$ag = new Phlickr_AuthedGroup($api, '78064184@N00');
```

You can find the ID for groups that you administer by clicking on a group's name from the group page. You will see the group ID at the end of the URL, for example, `http://www.flickr.com/groups/14157979@N00/`.

Next, we iterate over the photos stored in the `Phlickr_PhotoListIterator` object.

```
foreach ($pli->getPhotos() as $photo) {
```

For each photo stored in the iterator, we get the ID of the photo and attempt to add it to the group using the `add()` method of the `Phlickr_AuthedGroup` object.

```
$photoid = $photo->getId();
```

```
try {
  $ag->add($photoid);
  echo 'adding photo '. $photoid, "<br />";
  flush();
} catch (Exception $e) {
  echo 'Error: ', $e->getMessage(), "<br />";
  flush();
}
```

We use the `try` block because the API will throw an exception and the code will halt if the current photo is already in the group. We would like it to keep going with the other photos, despite the problem. Using the `try` block allows us to do just that. If the photo is not in the group, the photo is added; otherwise the error message is printed and the program continues on.

Adding a Tag to All the Photos in a Group

Now that our group has some photos, we can start building a website that will use the images. What we'd like to do is query Flickr and tell it to pull images from the group and show only images with a specific tag.

Try It Out: Adding a Tag to a Group

Unfortunately there is no way to query just a specific group, but we can work around this by assigning all the photos in the group a special tag that identifies them as a member of the group. You want to pick a tag that is unique and won't be used by other Flickr users. In this case, we are using the tag `ewwckfpool` to identify a photo as a member of the group. While we are at it, we'll also add the tags `kungfu` and `wingchun` in case someone in the group adds a photo that doesn't have these tags.

```php
<?php
//tag_photos_in_a_group.php

define('API_CONFIG_FILE', './authtoken.dat');

include_once 'Phlickr/Api.php';
include_once 'Phlickr/Group.php';
include_once 'Phlickr/PhotoListIterator.php';

// set up the api connection
$api = Phlickr_Api::createFrom(API_CONFIG_FILE);
if (! $api->isAuthValid()) {
  die("invalid flickr logon");
}

$script_filename = basename($_REQUEST['SCRIPT_FILENAME']);
$tags = $_REQUEST["tags"];
$group_id = $_REQUEST["groupid"];
?>

<html>
  <head>
    <title>Add Tags to all the photos in a Group</title>
  </head>

  <body>
    <form method='get' action='<?php echo $script_filename; ?>'>
      <p>enter a comma-separated list of tags
        <input type='text' name='tags' value='<?php echo $tags; ?>' />
        and enter the group id
        <input type='text' name='groupid' value='<?php echo $group_id; ?>' />
      </p>
      <input type='submit' value='Add a tag or tags to every photo in the group'/>
    </form>

    <?php
    if ($tags == '' or $group_id == '') {
      die('Please enter a tag or set of tags and a group id');
    }

    $group = new Phlickr_Group($api, $group_id);
    $photolist = $group->getPhotoList();

    $iterator = new Phlickr_PhotoListIterator($photolist);

    foreach ($iterator->getPhotos() as $photo) {
      $photo->addTags(explode( ',', $tags));
      echo "<br />";
```

```
      echo "adding tags to photo #".$photo->getId()."<br />";
      echo "the new tags are: <br />";
      foreach ($photo->getTags() as $tag) {
        echo $tag. "<br />";
      }
    }
    ?>
  </body>
</html>
```

When you view the page in a web browser, you will get something that looks like Figure 9-2.

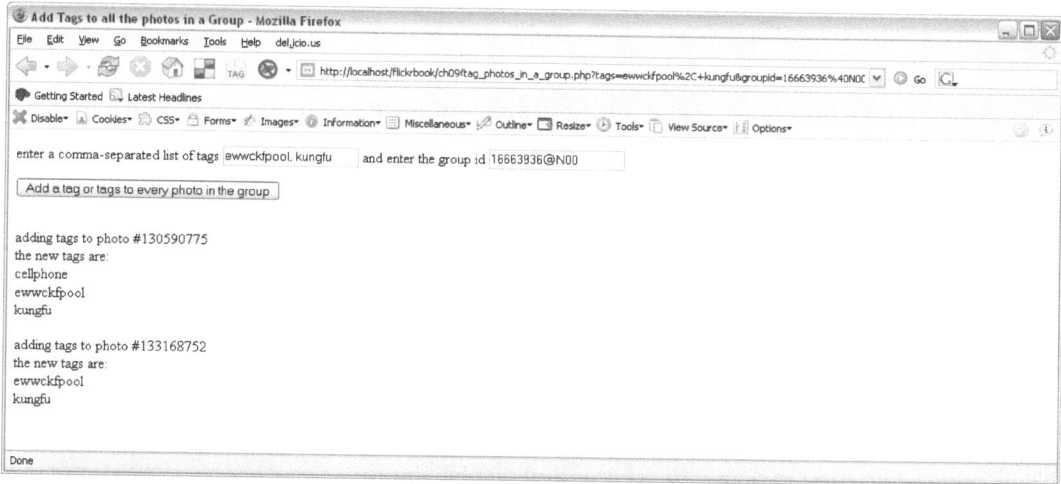

Figure 9-2. *Adding a tag to all the photos in a group*

Notice that the photos are now tagged with kungfu and ewwckfpool in addition to the tags that were already on the photos.

How It Works

This example is similar to a previous example where we added a tag to all of the photos in a specific set. In this case though, we are using a group for the source of photos rather than a set. To do this we use the Phlickr_Group class and set it to the group we've created.

```
$group = new Phlickr_Group($api, $group_id);
```

We create a Phlickr_PhotoList and set it to all of the photos in the group, using the getPhotoList() method of the Phlickr_Group object.

```
$photolist = $group->getPhotoList();
```

A photo list is a set of photos grouped in pages, much the way you view photos when looking at your photostream, showing only ten photos at a time. If we wanted to go through them all, we would have to work with ten photos, go to the next page, work with the next ten photos, and so on. The `Phlickr_PhotoListIterator` object simplifies this. Instead of groups of ten photos, the `Phlickr_PhotoListIterator` returns one long list of photos.

```
$iterator = new Phlickr_PhotoListIterator($photolist);
```

We can then iterate through the photos and add the new tags using the `addTags()` method of the `Phlickr_Photo` object.

```
foreach ($iterator->getPhotos() as $photo) {
  $photo->addTags(explode( ',', $tags));
  echo "<br />";
  echo "adding tags to photo #". $photo->getId()."<br />";
  echo "the new tags are: <br />";
  foreach ($photo->getTags() as $tag) {
    echo $tag. "<br />";
  }
}
```

We also write the photo ID and the list of tags out to the command window using the `echo` command.

Searching and Displaying the Group Photos

Now that we've made a special tag for all the photos in the group, we can easily search the photos and display them. To do this we'll modify the example we used in the previous chapter a little to serve our purposes here.

Try It Out: A Search Page

Following is the code to search for photos and display them:

```
<?php
//tag_search_page.php

define('API_CONFIG_FILE', './authtoken.dat');

require_once 'Phlickr/Api.php';
require_once 'Phlickr/PhotoList.php';
require_once 'Phlickr/PhotoListIterator.php';

// set up the api connection
$api = Phlickr_Api::createFrom(API_CONFIG_FILE);
if (! $api->isAuthValid()) {
  die("invalid flickr logon");
}

$script_filename = basename($_REQUEST['SCRIPT_FILENAME']);
$tags = $_REQUEST["tags"];
?>
```

```php
<html>
  <head>
    <title>East West Wing Chug Kung Fu Association Photo Tag Search</title>
  </head>

  <body>
    <div align="center">
      <h2>East West Wing Chug Kung Fu Association Photo Tag Search</h2>

      <form method='get' action='<?php echo $script_filename; ?>'>
        <p>Enter tags to search for, separated by commas
          <input type='text' name='tags' value='<?php echo $tags; ?>' />
        </p>
        <input type='submit' value='Find Photos'/>
      </form>
      <p>
        <?php
        $tags = $_REQUEST['tags'];
        $tags = $tags.", ewwckfpool";

        $request = $api->createRequest(
          'flickr.photos.search',
          array(
            'tags' => $tags,
            'tag_mode' => 'all'
          )
        );

        $pl = new Phlickr_PhotoList($request, Phlickr_PhotoList::PER_PAGE_MAX);
        $pli = new Phlickr_PhotoListIterator($pl);

        foreach ($pli->getPhotos() as $photo) {
          $photoid = $photo->getId();
        ?>

        <a href="<?php echo $photo->buildImgURL('o'); ?>">
          <img src="<?php echo $photo->buildImgURL('s'); ?>"/></a>

        <?php
          flush();
        }
        ?>
      </p>
    </div>
  </body>
</html>
```

The resulting web page will look something like Figure 9-3, depending on which tags you search for.

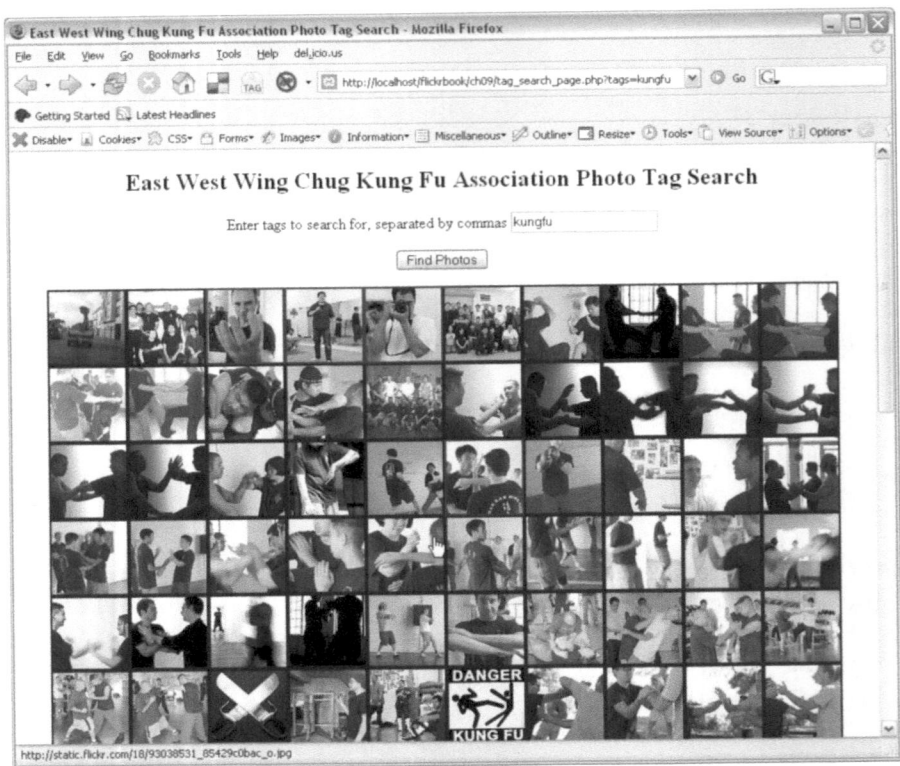

Figure 9-3. *Searching group photos with tags*

How It Works

Here we've embedded some PHP code into a web page. We use a simple HTML form to submit our query and the $_REQUEST superglobal variable to retrieve the submission, as we did in the previous chapter.

```
$tags = $_REQUEST['tags'];
```

However, in this example, we add to the query our special tag that identifies photos in the group. In this case, we used ewwckfpool.

```
$tags = $tags." ewwckfpool";
```

Now when the search is performed, it will show only the group photos that have been tagged with the special identifier.

Displaying a Random Image from a Group

One problem with photos in Flickr groups is that they tend to get lost. As new photos are added to the group, the older ones get pushed somewhere in the middle of the group. If they aren't tagged and searchable, they tend to disappear. One way to make these images more visible is to display a random image on a web page.

Try It Out: A Random Photo

Following is the code that will display a random photo for us:

```php
<?php
//random_photo.php

define('API_CONFIG_FILE', './authtoken.dat');

include_once 'Phlickr/Api.php';
include_once 'Phlickr/Group.php';
include_once 'Phlickr/PhotoListIterator.php';

$script_filename= basename($_REQUEST['SCRIPT_FILENAME']);

$api = Phlickr_Api::createFrom(API_CONFIG_FILE);
if (! $api->isAuthValid()) {
  die("invalid flickr logon");
}

$group = new Phlickr_Group($api, '14157979@N00');
$photolist = $group->getPhotoList();

// iterate over all the pages
$iterator = new Phlickr_PhotoListIterator($photolist);
$photos = $iterator->getPhotos();

$randomnumber = rand(1,count($photos));
?>

<html>
  <head>
    <title>Random Photo</title>
    <meta http-equiv="Refresh" content="10; url=<?php echo $script_filename; ?>"/>
  </head>

  <body style="vertical-align:middle; text-align:center">
    <img src="<?php echo $photos[$randomnumber]->buildImgUrl('-'); ?>"
         alt="A random image"/>
  </body>
</html>
```

When you open the web page, you will see a random image from your group as shown in Figure 9-4. The page will reload automatically, and you will see an updated image.

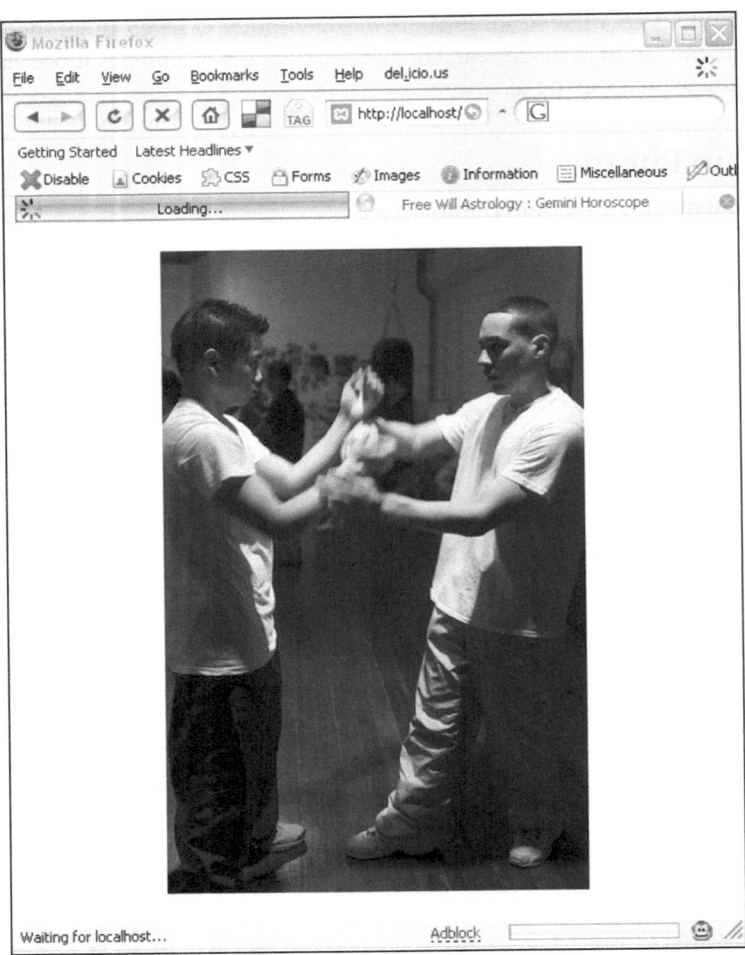

Figure 9-4. *Random group image page*

How It Works

The beginning of the code for this example is similar to the first example, where we tagged all the photos in a group. We open an API connection and get all the group photos using the Phlickr_Group class and the Phlickr_PhotoListIterator. Instead of going through all the images, this time we use PHP's rand() function to pick a random photo from the group.

```
$randomnumber = rand(1,count($photos));
```

Once we've picked a random photo, we simply display it in a web page. In this case we used a table so the image would display neatly in the middle of the page. Notice the META tag in the following HTML output:

```
<meta http-equiv="Refresh" content="10; url=<?php echo $script_filename; ?>"/>
```

This causes the page to reload every ten seconds, pulling a new random image from the group.

Displaying Recent Posts to a Group on an External Web Page

In our last chapter we learned about the different RSS feeds produced by Flickr and how to call the URL for an RSS feed from different Phlickr objects.

Up to this point we've avoided using anything other than the Phlickr library and PHP itself for examples, just to keep things easy. In this example we will use the MagpieRSS parser library to parse Flickr feeds. MagpieRSS is an easy-to-use, state-of-the-art PHP library for reading RSS feeds.

Fortunately, getting and installing the MagpieRSS libraries is very simple. You can download the latest version from SourceForge at: http://magpierss.sourceforge.net/.

Next, you simply unzip the file to the directory where you have the Phlickr libraries installed. So say you have Phlickr installed at: c:\php\pear\Phlickr. For this example, you need to unzip MagpieRSS into a folder called c:\php\pear\magpierss. It's that simple.

In order use MagpieRSS, you will need know a little bit about the feed that you are going to parse. In this case, we are going to parse the discussion feed for a Flickr group, so before we go any further, we will need to take a look at that feed. Let's take a look at the feed for the Flickr Central group. The URL for the group feed is http://flickr.com/groups_feed.gne?id=34427469792@N01&format=atom.

Remember that any group feed can be accessed this way by changing the ID in the URL to the ID of the group in question. We specified here that we want the feed in Atom format, which returns an Atom 0.3 feed, which we worked with in the previous chapter.

Try It Out: Parsing an RSS Feed

Now that we know the layout of the feed, we'll know what to look for when we begin parsing with MagpieRSS. Let's take a quick look at what MagpieRSS does when we supply it with the feed from a Flickr group.

```php
<?php
//print_rss.php

require 'magpierss/rss_fetch.inc';
$rss =
  fetch_rss('http://flickr.com/groups_feed.gne?id=34427469792@N01&format=atom');
print_r ($rss);
?>
```

When you run this on the command line, you will get a long complex array that begins something like the following:

```
$ php print_rss.php
```

```
MagpieRSS Object
(
    [parser] => 0
    [current_item] => Array
        (
        )

    [items] => Array
        (
            [0] => Array
                (
                    [title] => Reply to flickr coincidence
                    [link] => http://www.flickr.com/groups/central/discuss/12809/
                        1455599/
                    [id] => tag:flickr.com,2005:/groupcomment/72157594149868965
                    [published] => 2006-05-30T15:51:44Z
                    [updated] => 2006-05-30T15:51:44Z
                    [atom_content] => <p>
<a href="http://www.flickr.com/people/bluheron/">bluheron</a> posted a reply:</p>
    ...
```

How It Works

For this example we're using MagpieRSS, so we need to include the rss_fetch library in the beginning of our script, as well as the Phlickr libraries.

```
require 'magpierss/rss_fetch.inc';
```

We instruct MagpieRSS to go to Flickr and get the Atom feed using the fetch_rss() method and return it to the command line using print_r().

```
$rss =
  fetch_rss('http://flickr.com/groups_feed.gne?id=34427469792@N01&format=atom');
```

As you can see, the fetch_rss() method returned a parsed version of the feed, with the parts broken out into a set of nested arrays. Two arrays of particular interest to us are the [items] array and the [channel] array (not shown in the preceding code). The former stores a set of posts and replies to the group. The [channel] array stores the title, link, and description of the entire feed.

Try It Out: Displaying RSS Data

Since the feed is now parsed and put neatly into arrays, we can put the arrays to use.

```php
<?php
//read_feed.php

define('API_CONFIG_FILE', './authtoken.dat');

require_once 'Phlickr/Api.php';
require_once 'Phlickr/AuthedGroup.php';
require_once 'magpierss/rss_fetch.inc';

$api = Phlickr_Api::createFrom(API_CONFIG_FILE);
if (! $api->isAuthValid()) {
  die("invalid flickr logon");
}

$ag = new Phlickr_AuthedGroup($api, '34427469792@N01');
$groupfeed = $ag->buildDiscussFeedUrl("atom");

$discuss_atom = fetch_rss($groupfeed);

$feed = $discuss_atom->channel;

echo 'Group Title:'.$feed['title']."<br />";
echo 'Group Link:'.$feed['link']."<br />";

echo "<br />";
echo 'Group Description:'.strip_tags($feed['subtitle'])."<br />";
echo "<br />";

foreach ($discuss_atom->items as $feeditem) {
  echo ' Feed Item--->'.$feeditem['title']."<br />";
}
?>
```

If you look at this in a browser, you will see something similar to Figure 9-5.

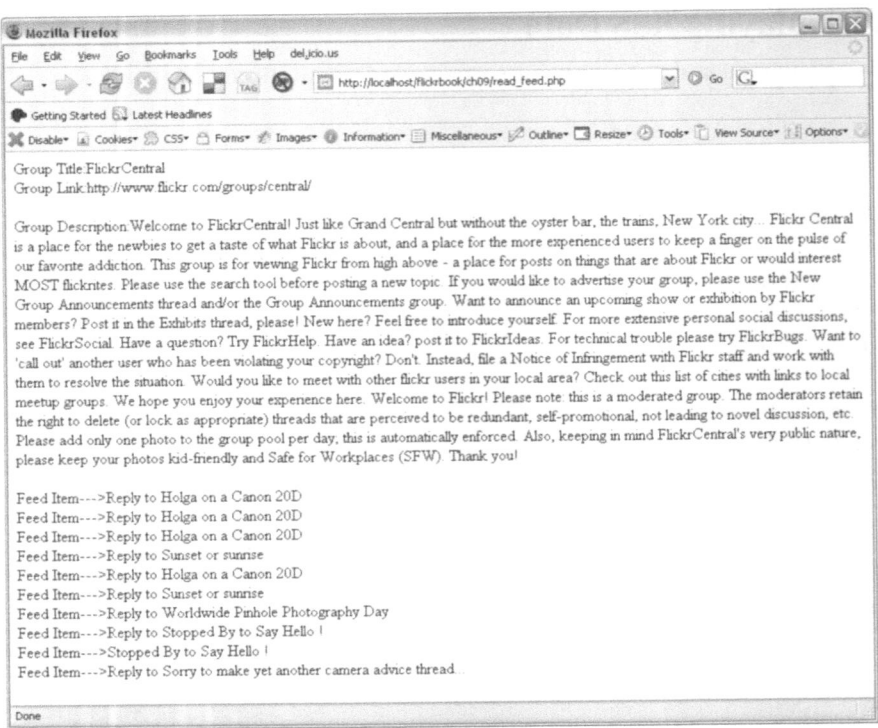

Figure 9-5. *Collapsed Atom feed from a Flickr group*

How It Works

Again, in this example we are using MagpieRSS, so you'll need to include it along with the Phlickr libraries we will be using.

```
require_once 'Phlickr/Api.php';
require_once 'Phlickr/AuthedGroup.php';
require_once 'magpierss/rss_fetch.inc';
```

Next, we create a new Phlickr_Group object and set it to the Flickr Central group. We use the Phlickr_Group object to return the location of the RSS feed we want and store that in the variable $groupfeed.

```
$ag = new Phlickr_AuthedGroup($api, '34427469792@N01');
$groupfeed = $ag->buildDiscussFeedUrl("atom"));
```

From there use MagpieRSS to grab the actual RSS feed from Flickr and store it in the $discuss_atom variable.

```
$discuss_atom = fetch_rss($groupfeed);
```

We create a new variable called $feed, which stores an array of feed information provided by MagpieRSS. Notice that we specify the channel array using the -> symbol.

```
$feed = $discuss_atom->channel;
```

We then can echo the parts of the channel array to the command line using standard array notation. Notice that we use the PHP strip_tags() function to remove the HTML tags stored in the description.

```
echo 'Group Title:'.$feed['title']."<br />";
echo 'Group Link:'.$feed['link']."<br />";

echo "<br />";
echo 'Group Description:'.strip_tags($feed['subtitle'])."<br />";
echo "<br />";
```

Finally, we iterate over the individual feed items, and echo the titles to the screen.

```
foreach ($discuss_atom->items as $feeditem) {
  echo ' Feed Item--->'.$feeditem['title']."<br />";
}
```

Try It Out: A Prettier Version

Since this chapter is about building pages that you can add to your website, let's take this example and make a proper web page out of it.

To begin with, we'll make a simple cascading style sheet (CSS) that will give our page an interesting look.

```
body {
  font: 8pt/16pt georgia;
  color: #555753;
  margin: 15px;
}

h1 {
  font: 20pt georgia;
  text-align:center;
  border: 1px solid black;
  background-color: cccccc;
}

p.new {
  font-weight: bold;
  padding: 5px;
  border: 1px solid black;
}
```

```css
div.topic {
  padding: 10px;
  border: 1px solid black;
  background-color: cccccc;
  margin-left: 20px;
}

a:link {
  font-weight: bold;
  text-decoration: none;
  color: #9685BA;
}

a:visited {
  font-weight: bold;
  text-decoration: none;
  color: #B7A5DF;
}

a:hover, a:active {
  text-decoration: underline;
}
```

This code should be saved in the same directory as the next piece of code, with the file name feed.css.

Next, we'll adapt our previous example to use proper HTML.

```php
<?php
//feed_page.php

define('API_CONFIG_FILE', './authtoken.dat');

require_once 'Phlickr/Api.php';
require_once 'Phlickr/AuthedGroup.php';
require_once 'magpierss/rss_fetch.inc';

$api = Phlickr_Api::createFrom(API_CONFIG_FILE);
if (! $api->isAuthValid()) {
  die("invalid flickr logon");
}

$ag = new Phlickr_AuthedGroup($api, '34427469792@N01');
$groupfeed = $ag->buildDiscussFeedUrl("atom");

$discuss_atom = fetch_rss($groupfeed);
```

```php
$feed = $discuss_atom->channel;
?>

<html>
  <head>
    <title>Group Feed Example</title>
    <style type="text/css" media="all">
      @import "feed.css";
    </style>
  </head>

  <body>
    <a href="<?php echo $feed['link']; ?>">
      <h1><?php echo $feed['title']; ?></h1>
    </a>

    <p><?php echo $feed['subtitle']; ?></p>

    <h2>Recent Topics</h2>

    <?php
    foreach ($discuss_atom->items as $item){
      if (substr($item['title'], 0, 5) != 'Reply') {
    ?>

    <p class="new">New Topic:
      <a href="<?php echo $item['link']; ?>"><?php echo $item['title']; ?></a>
    </p>

    <div class="topic"><?php echo $item['atom_content']; ?></div>

    <?php
      }
    }
    ?>

    <h2>Recent Replies to Previous Topics</h2>

    <?php
    foreach ($discuss_atom->items as $item) {
      if (substr($item['title'], 0, 5) == 'Reply') {
    ?>

    <p class="new">New Reply:
      <a href="<?php echo $item['link']; ?>"><?php echo $item['title']; ?></a>
    </p>
```

```
<div class="topic"><?php echo $item['atom_content']; ?></div><br/>

<?php
    }
}
?>
</body>
</html>
```

When you open this page in a web browser, you will see a web page that gives the group title and description, followed by the recent topics and recent replies, as shown in Figure 9-6.

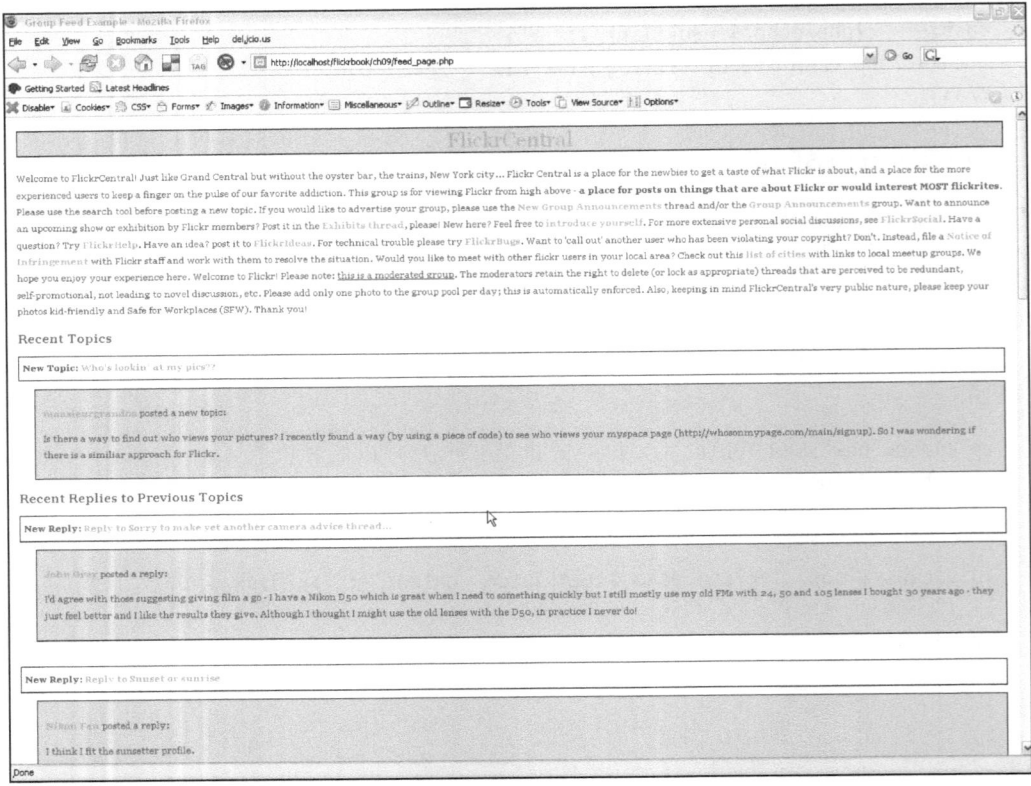

Figure 9-6. *Recent posts to a group on an external web page*

How It Works

In this example, we've taken the result from MagpieRSS and formatted them with HTML tags. As in our last example, we include the libraries we will need, then instruct MagpieRSS to fetch the feed URL and return the values in an array. We then take the feed information and put it at the top of the page.

```
<a href="<?php echo $feed['link']; ?>">
  <h1><?php echo $feed['title']; ?></h1>
</a>

<p><?php echo $feed['subtitle']; ?></p>
```

We then iterate through the items twice. The first time we iterate through, we check to see whether the item is a topic as opposed to a reply. Notice that the titles of all replies begin "Reply to…." In order to tell whether an item is a reply, we check the first couple of characters of the item title to see whether it begins with "Reply." We do this using the PHP `substr()` function. If the title does not begin with "Reply," we return it to the browser, formatted with HTML tags.

```
<h2>Recent Topics</h2>

<?php
foreach ($discuss_atom->items as $item){
  if (substr($item['title'], 0, 5) != 'Reply') {
?>

<p class="new">New Topic:
  <a href="<?php echo $item['link']; ?>"><?php echo $item['title']; ?></a>
</p>

<div class="topic"><?php echo $item['atom_content']; ?></div>

<?php
  }
}
?>
```

Note that the contents of an Atom feed's entry are available in the `atom_content` attribute of the item's array.

Similarly, the second time we iterate through the replies, we look for items that do have "Reply" as the leftmost five characters:

```
if (substr($item['title'], 0, 5) == 'Reply') {
```

Notice also that if the resulting web page already has hyperlinks included, you may see images that people have linked to in their posts. If for some reason you want the HTML links removed, you can do so using the PHP `strip_tags()` function to remove any unwanted HTML links.

Try It Out: Latest Group Images

In addition to pulling the latest comments to the group, we can also look at the latest photos added to the group.

```php
<?php
//latest_photos.php

define('API_CONFIG_FILE', './authtoken.dat');

include_once 'Phlickr/Api.php';
include_once 'Phlickr/AuthedGroup.php';
include_once 'Phlickr/Photo.php';
include_once 'magpierss/rss_fetch.inc';

$api = Phlickr_Api::createFrom(API_CONFIG_FILE);
if (! $api->isAuthValid()) {
  die("invalid flickr logon");
}

$ag = new Phlickr_AuthedGroup($api, '78064184@N00');
$photo_atom = fetch_rss($ag->buildPhotoFeedUrl("atom"));
?>

<html>
  <head>
    <title>Latest Group Images</title>
  </head>

  <body>
    <h2>Latest Group Images</h2>

    <?php
    foreach ($photo_atom->items as $item) {
      $patharray = explode('/', $item['link']);
      $photo_id = $patharray[5];
      $photo = new Phlickr_Photo ($api, $photo_id);
    ?>

    <a href="<?php echo $item['link']; ?>">
      <img src="<?php echo $photo->buildImgUrl('s'); ?>"
           alt="<?php echo $item['title']; ?>" />
    <?php
    }
    ?>
  </body>
</html>
```

When you open this file in a web browser, you will see square thumbnails of the latest ten images that were added to the group, as shown in Figure 9-7.

Figure 9-7. *Thumbnails of the last ten images posted to a group*

How It Works

This time, instead of building the discussion URL, we use the `buildPhotoFeedUrl()` method of the `Phlickr_Group` object. This returns a feed URL that we pass to MagpieRSS.

```
$photo_atom = fetch_rss($ag->buildPhotoFeedUrl("atom"));
```

In this case, the results returned by MagpieRSS are similar to those we saw before, except that the title returned in this case is the photo title, and the link returned is a link to the photo page. The feed doesn't, however, return the photo ID separately. In order to make a thumbnail of an image, we need the photo ID to create a photo object. Fortunately, the photo ID is stored inside of the URL to the photo page. To get it we use the PHP `explode()` function.

```
$patharray = explode('/', $item['link']);
$photo_id = $patharray[5];
```

The `explode()` function works by breaking down a string into smaller parts by using a certain character as the delimiter. For instance, a photo URL might look like the following:

```
http://www.flickr.com/photos/oneupmanshipwreck/31313582/in/pool-eastwest/
```

What we want is the photo ID, in this case 31313582. If we break this URL up using the / character, we would have an array that has nine items:

```
Array ( [0] => http: [1] => [2] => www.flickr.com [3] => photos [4] =>
  oneupmanshipwreck [5] => 31313582 [6] => in [7] => pool-eastwest [8] => )
```

What we want is array item number 5, the photo id. Once we have the ID, we build the image URL and format the results in HTML tags.

Summary

In this chapter we've looked at ways to use Flickr as the back end to your collaborative website. The examples here demonstrate how you can get your group photos and put them to use. Each of these examples can be easily dropped into an existing website to add collaborative functionality. Hopefully we've sparked your imagination with some of the limitless possibilities for ways that you can add color and collaboration to your group website.

Index

You Need the Companion eBook

Your purchase of this book entitles you to buy the companion PDF-version eBook for only $10. Take the weightless companion with you anywhere.

We believe this Apress title will prove so indispensable that you'll want to carry it with you everywhere, which is why we are offering the companion eBook (in PDF format) for $10 to customers who purchase this book now. Convenient and fully searchable, the PDF version of any content-rich, page-heavy Apress book makes a valuable addition to your programming library. You can easily find and copy code — or perform examples by quickly toggling between instructions and the application. Even simultaneously tackling a donut, diet soda, and complex code becomes simplified with hands-free eBooks!

Once you purchase your book, getting the $10 companion eBook is simple:

❶ Visit **www.apress.com/promo/tendollars/**.

❷ Complete a basic registration form to receive a randomly generated question about this title.

❸ Answer the question correctly in 60 seconds, and you will receive a promotional code to redeem for the $10.00 eBook.

2560 Ninth Street • Suite 219 • Berkeley, CA 94710

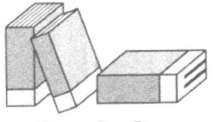

eBookshop

THE EXPERT'S VOICE™